TAKEN FOR A RIDE

"If there really is a better way than PPP, why has the Mayor's office singularly failed to come forward with a detailed workable alternative capable of immediate implementation at no risk to the UK taxpayer?"
– Digby Jones, Director General, CBI

T0270128

TAKEN FOR A RIDE

Second Edition

Taxpayers, Trains and HM Treasury

Don Riley with
Fred Harrison, Jonathan Brown and
Dave Wetzel

SHEPHEARD-WALWYN (PUBLISHERS) LTD

First published in 2001 by
the *Centre for Land Policy Studies*

Second Edition 2024, published by
the *Centre for Land Policy Studies*
www.wearerent.com
with
Shepheard-Walwyn (Publishers) Ltd
107 Parkway House, Sheen Lane, London SW14 8LS

British Library Cataloguing in Publication Data

A catalogue record is available from the British Library.

Paperback ISBN 978-1-916517-03-5 (2nd Edition)
eBook ISBN 978-1-916517-04-2 (2nd Edition)

www.shepheardwalwyn.com

Cover design by Andrew Candy www.tentacledesign.co.uk
Printed and bound in the United Kingdom by 4edge Ltd

Contents

Original Foreword

I dedicate this book to the builders of the Jubilee Line Extension – the employees and sub-contractors of Costain/Taylor Woodrow joint venture, Contract 104, Jubilee Line at London Bridge.

They occupied the spare buildings of ours that were rented for offices, changing rooms and showers for engineers and miners during 1995–1999. Early on they earned my respect for their energy and enthusiasm.

Later I appreciated their grit and determination when I trudged the newly-dug dusty tunnel between the Thames and Blackfriars Bridge Road. Now, in 2001, as I watch the activity on the surface around Bankside, I remember what they risked and achieved below ground.

It is with gratitude that I register my admiration for their contribution to the resulting above-ground property revival and rocketing prices in this area.

When I came to appreciate their efforts for land owners along the Jubilee Line, and on my behalf I ended up more embarrassed than smug.

But most of them did not have a clue as to where their next job would be.

This book is dedicated to their efforts, and to showing that a better way exists to provide transport infrastructure that would ensure their skills were continuously in demand.

Don Riley
London
May 2001

Foreword to the 2024 Edition

Shepheard-Walwyn is proud to collaborate with the Centre for Land Policy Studies to publish a revised edition of the classic book, *Taken for a Ride* – a book that has had an important impact on UK transport policy in general, and London transport in particular.

Revising any book presents difficult choices on what to change and what to leave alone. In this case, the quality of the first edition made most of these choices straightforward. Don Riley's arguments have been confirmed repeatedly in the 22 years since publication. Consequently, we have chosen to leave the original text unchanged.

To update the work, we have added context and additional insight at the end of each chapter. We have reviewed predictions and printed what actually happened. In almost all the cases, the author's predictions have been confirmed. If there is a fault in Don's work, it has been in underestimating the extraordinary land value increase that was made possible by the Jubilee Line Extension (JLE).We also have a new introduction from Fred Harrison, the original series editor and the UK's most important land and business cycles economist and a new postscript by Dave Wetzel, former vice chair of Transport for London. Dave is especially qualified to talk about the impact of Don's work and the work still to do. Dave has spent his life working to improve transport in and around London and even in official retirement still campaigns tirelessly for a fairer economy and more prosperous society.

Steven Norris, the transport minister who finally won funding for the JLE in 1995, has also kindly contributed a behind-the-scenes view of the tortuous approval process. In uncompromising detail, he shares exactly what it took to get the Treasury to make what has turned out to be one of the best public investments in modern times. That the gains have gone to the private landowners, instead of being used to transform the rest of our failing infrastructure, is one of the key points of this book.

One final change is the addition of more photographs showing the places that Don owned and wrote about. The buildings themselves add to Don's work and so we are pleased that advances in publishing mean we can make them a bigger part of the story.

Jonathan Brown, London, January 2024.

2024 Introduction
Fred Harrison

I have been involved with many books over the years that strive to create a fairer and more dynamic economic system. Working with Don Riley to produce *Taken for a Ride* was most enjoyable and rewarding. Don's story resonates with people from all political persuasions, which is why Shepheard-Walwyn are issuing a revised edition over 22 years after its publication.

Don Riley was a New Zealand born entrepreneur who began buying property and land in and around London Bridge in the 1970s. Initially, this was to house his own employees but given his skills and how much he enjoyed improving buildings, it eventually became his main business. He was committed to the area and had a front row seat when the Thatcher government decided to extend the Jubilee underground railway from Waterloo Station to the new financial centre in Docklands. Several of his commercial buildings were within a few yards of the holes dug beneath what would become the Jubilee Line tube or Underground stations in Southwark. He not only monitored the progress, but even went below ground to watch the boring of the tunnels. He wanted to chart the impact on the rents he could charge his tenants. What he found conformed to an almost forgotten and mostly ignored economic theory, The Ricardian Theory of Rent (more of this later in the book).

Don found that the closer to the completion date, the greater the increase in rents, which could be attributed to the Jubilee extension. Properties located further away from the station featured lower increases in rents. Riley was pleased to monitor the unfolding events in real time. He was not pleased, however, with the fact that he could make more money out of owning land than rehabilitating old buildings.

Don's research and his attacks on what he deemed to be a deeply unfair tax system was surprisingly influential and struck a chord with many people from across the political spectrum. I think there were a number of reasons why this book resonated so much. Firstly, who would not be intrigued to hear from an entrepreneur turned property developer complain about making too much money from his property investments? And then goading the government to do something about it – namely change the tax system?

Don't get me wrong, Don was a committed entrepreneur and worked to maximise his profits. He did it in a creative and thoughtful way as many of his developments showed, but he wasn't a socialist entrepreneur – far from it. What he hated was unfairness and unjust outcomes. He also knew intuitively (and then financially) that distortions in economic systems – especially incentives and disincentives – hurt everyone, even those they seemingly benefit (the landowners). To him, seeing his investments increase dramatically simply because a government had decided to spend public money to build an underground station within 400m of his properties, was an afront to his entrepreneurial spirit. He also knew that it could easily prevent him acting in his and others' best interests.

In the chapter entitled 'The Gravy Train', he speaks about Rule No.1, which drives the markets for labour and capital: "*people pay for the benefits they receive*". As this book showed so clearly, that's not the case in the land and property markets. Finding ways to ensure we all pay for what we receive would make markets more efficient but also much fairer. In that way, we stop punishing people for doing the right thing. Under the current tax regime, people *are* punished for generating benefits in the marketplace.

Don understood what really drove an economy and community forward was ensuring people were encouraged to work hard AND be rewarded fairly for that hard work. At one point in the book, he castigates politicians for underpaying public sector workers who had done so much to improve a community, but who were then priced out of their home communities because their pay increases failed to keep up with housing costs. How can we build communities if the people who help create them can't afford to live in them? For Don, this was an example of people creating benefits for the economy *and* being punished for doing so.

If a reader failed to understand Don's perspective on fair rewards, Don might be perceived as the proverbial turkey voting for Christmas. This is utterly wrong. Indeed, it is a deep regret of my career that Don's mindset is not more widely held and that instead many see in these pages a picture of Don Riley, eccentric investor.

That Don was often seen as eccentric shows how far our society and economic system have fallen from authentic capitalism and entrepreneurship. We now have more people at the top of the economic tree taking gains who did little or nothing to achieve them and narcissistically claiming credit for that gain. In short, our biggest economic problem is the same economic problem first articulated by the classical economists nearly 300 years ago – free-riding.

If Adam Smith, a founding member of classical economics, had met Don Riley he would have recognised him as the very entrepreneur he envisioned in *The Wealth of Nations*.

Adam Smith, the political economist, would have rejoiced at seeing a man committed to finding unmet needs in his community and using all his entrepreneurial flair and creativity to meet those needs *and be rewarded for doing so*.

Adam Smith, the moral philosopher, would also have recognised Don as a man embodying many of the finest traits described in his other, perhaps more important work, *A Theory of Moral Sentiments*. Don had a legendary commitment to fairness and justice, and you can see it running throughout the book.

My first challenge is to ask why, when Don's philosophy was the very essence of the enlightened self-interest as described by Adam Smith, regarded as the Father of Capitalism, do we find Don's ideas relegated to the margins of political and economic debates? Aren't we supposed to be a capitalist economy? What does this tell us about the real problems with "capitalism" as we know it today?

In the twenty or so years following the publication of *Taken for a Ride*, a number of professional surveys were commissioned which confirmed Don's results. There is one incontestable conclusion: *if the Thatcher government had collected the increase in location values, it would have been possible to fund the Jubilee infrastructure without taxing wageworkers who lived hundreds of miles away from London, and who would not benefit from the new transit system.*

The most recent UK example of studies supporting Don's research is a study by Transport for London (TfL) with research conducted by management consultant KPMG, and Savills, one of the world's top property agents. The study proposed alternative ways to fund the development of new capital projects in London and Southeast England. Entitled "Land Value Capture", it was published in 2017 when cost overruns and delays to the Crossrail project (now the Elizabeth Line) were causing controversy – the same controversy Don proved to be untrue in his book – that major rail projects do not pay for themselves.

KPMG and Savills economists confirmed Don's assertion that you could capture the gains enjoyed by the land by mapping the value increases. Research in the report sought to value the gains from eight current and upcoming capital projects. This was their headline in the Executive Summary:

"Eight prospective TfL projects that cost around £36bn (including Crossrail 2 . . .) could produce land value uplifts of about £87bn.

The study also follows Don's example of mapping the rippling value uplift from a station. They begin with a 2014 study by the Nationwide Building Society Housing Survey. This shows the average increases from all major stations (Figure 1).

Savills also drew data from the Land Registry to show the cumulative gains of new projects. They measured gains from one year before construction to 5 years after completion.

Don's data, experience, and bank balance tell us that, for the stations closest to his properties, these gains were understated. But even as an average across all the stations, the gain from the Jubilee Line was impressive.

In explaining the value differential between projects, their reasoning also supports Don's experience and reflection as recorded in this book.

Figure 1 – The `transport premium' in London property prices

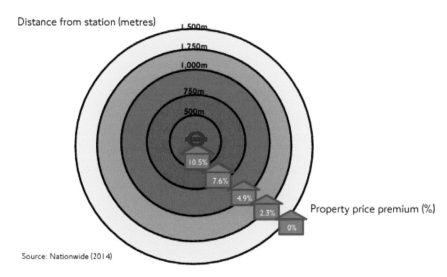

Distance from station (metres)

Property price premium (%)

Source: Nationwide (2014)

Figure 2 – Total residential value uplift around historic case study projects

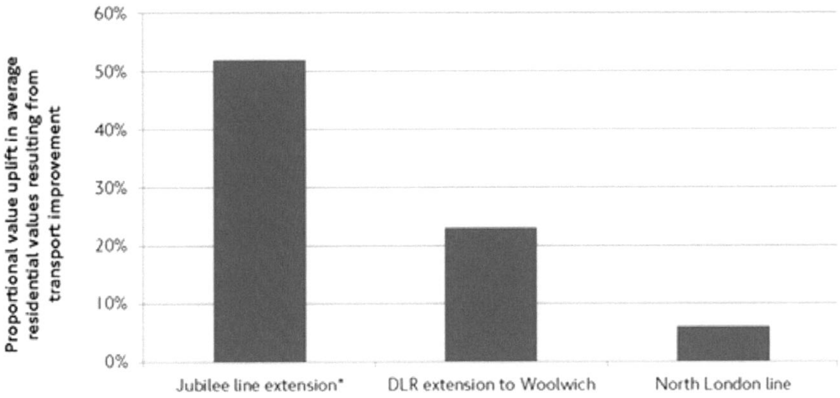

Source: Savills analysis for TfL; Land Registry

* Excludes stations with low sample sizes of property transactions

Proximity to already affluent areas, access to good jobs, opportunity to develop current (lower density) housing stock, and commercial interests, were all there on the Jubilee Line and in Don's research. The data proves that the Jubilee Line in general, and Don's stations in particular, have been some of the most successful projects anywhere in the world in the last 30 years for positive economic impact. Consequently, it's even more disappointing that we were not able to capture a fairer split of the gains to pay for the development and to finance other worthwhile projects.

The TfL findings also lend weight to Don's proposal that capital projects should be created to increase the land value (which would be shared by the community to build further prosperity). This is because, to maximise the uplift you must consider the community, and find ways to increase economic activity (and prosperity) and thoughtfully develop the space around the stations – projects Don always tried to achieve with his developments. Don describes the unusual approach he took to developing a site with a unique wood-framed building, but he only briefly mentions one of his greatest transformations, the former electrical factory (mentioned in Chapter 2) where he opened the Menier Chocolate Factory Theatre in 2004.

What is not surprising about the TfL report is that it falls short of Don's recommended solutions. They discuss an approach called

Development Rights Auction Model. From our position, whilst this would not go far enough, DRAM does seek to create a more collaborative approach to developing sites around new train stations, and encourage entrepreneurial activity. It also seeks to "encourage" those who do not want to do the work to take their profits and go. Their aim was to achieve devolved powers so that London could finance its own development projects.

There are links to these reports in the notes. They offer updates to many of the countries Don and I focused on in the book in the early 2000s.

The final reason this book deserves a new audience is that the solutions Don suggests are even more necessary today than they were over 20 years ago. It does not take too much investigation to see that we need to navigate a series of existential crises that are rapidly converging. Social, economic and political systems need to be integrated on the basis of a new paradigm. Deliberation on how to accomplish this has barely started. Governments and international agencies are largely content with proclaiming targets, such as Zero Emissions, without providing convincing plans for achieving the goals. For example, the climate crisis outcomes will fall far short of the targets. This will amplify the related global traumas instead of bringing them under control. These include food shortages in the Global South which will spur forced migrations, autocracy and militarism in the East leading to violent ethnic conflicts, and policy paralysis in the democratic West.

Taken for a Ride offers a way to reimagine transport systems in ways that are still relevant today. Over the past two centuries, mass transit systems have contributed enormously to the environmental crisis. At the same time, transportation can be a core element of sustainable solutions. *Taken for a Ride* illustrates the issues in the sphere of economics and high finance.

Plans for realigning future transport systems need to engage with three key issues.

- *Funding*: with most nations buckling under massive sovereign debts, how will highways and transit technologies be funded? The privatisation model deployed by the Thatcher government in the UK amplified rather than diminished the financial problems.
- *Politics*: how will governments mobilise democratic support for the enormous challenges that are required? The tax burden has

diminished public trust in the decision-making powers of policymakers. Does a benign revenue-raising strategy exist?

- *Ecology*: myriad problems are linked to transit systems, from pollution in urban areas (which is now known to kill people), to the scattering of communities as people rely increasingly on their own cars, rather than public transport.

The solution to the funding issue is revealed in forensic detail in this monograph. We need to apply the lessons to the challenges of the 21st century. In addition to the funding problem, other issues arise, as revealed by a revolutionary approach to mass transit promoted by Tesla entrepreneur Elon Musk in the USA. Among his ingenious innovations is the technology for boring tunnels beneath scattered metropolitan areas. The new linkages would cut travel times and reduce carbon emissions.[1] A 1.7-mile loop beneath the Las Vegas Convention Center proved that tunnels could be bored in record time, and at lower cost to the methods employed in creating London's Jubilee underground.

The Boring Company is aiming for 55 stations along a tunnel network beneath the casino city. Passengers would be ferried across the city in a fleet of Tesla cars, benefitting the environment. There are inevitable consequences to this.

The high-tech ingenuity of entrepreneurs like Musk results in a by-product: an increase in the net gains from innovations like carbon-free transit systems. The net gains in aggregate productivity surface as increases in location values. These translate into higher house prices. Under the current fiscal regime, that means more homelessness for those who cannot afford the price of dwellings; and family budgets stretched to breaking point by mortgages. Congestion on the highways may be reduced, but the price paid is an increase in congestion in the real estate sector; and increases in the ripple effects, such as the impact on mental health. The form of governance that authorises such outcomes increasingly depend on debt to fund public services.

Comprehensive audits are required before the Musk model is adopted in other cities – Austin, Miami, and Fort Lauderdale are being touted for the Boring project. People and agencies undertaking infrastructure

---

[1] https://www.boringcompany.com/projects

projects should include the deadweight losses in their calculations, not just the positive gains. By this means, rational decisions may be made on the overall impact on society and on the natural habitats occupied by people and the other species with whom we share Mother Earth.

Whilst Musk's ideas are utterly futuristic, deploying incredible imagination and the very latest technology, they are being applied within the context of a 200-year-old fiscal problem that is not being addressed. The solution that would allow everyone to benefit from true entrepreneurial activity is documented in *Taken for a Ride*.

In Britain, rehabilitating cities outside London will not be possible without enormous investment in new transit systems. Productivity is well below the potential for cities like Manchester and Birmingham because of the failure to connect people in scattered districts. This costs the UK an estimated £25bn in lost revenue every year.[2]

Funding the infrastructure, however, is just one element of the problem of under-performance. Availability of affordable housing is a related issue. People are driven out of city centres by high prices. This increases commuting time and costs, and contributes to lower value added to the economy. Again, the solution is in the rents generated by the rational planning of urban spaces. Thus, land used for farming is worth £10,000 an acre; that value leaps to £1m an acre, once permission has been granted to construct homes on it.[3] The uplift in value should be reserved to fund the social infrastructure (including the roads) which make communities liveable.

The holistic approach to reform is needed. *Taken for a Ride* provides important insights into the methodology needed for cleaning up the errors of the past and charting a new course into the future.

Fred Harrison
London
January 2024

---

[2] Amy Borrett (2023), Why do some UK cities punch below their weight? *Financial Times*, June 30.
[3] Emma Duncan 92023), "Starmer knows houses can rebuild economy", *The Times*, June 30.

Chapter 1

The Big Lie

For a lie to be converted into conventional wisdom, it is necessary for people in authority to keep repeating the falsehood. Repetition succeeds in blurring the distinction between fact and fiction. Governments can promote a lie by mobilising their bureaucracies to conceal the evidence. The lie becomes legitimate.

The Big Lie that we will expose affects every taxpayer in Britain today. It enables governments to damage the quality of our lives, and it empowers politicians to control people in a way that we would censure if it was going on under a Red Flag in a Communist country.

The Big Lie is at the heart of Britain's transport policy. It was repeated by the government's Strategic Rail Authority (SRA) in the document that is supposed to lay out an agenda for reform of the railway network. At the heart of the problem is the question of *who pays*. This is what the SRA boldly asserted as gospel:

> Again and again there will be choices between what the user must pay, what the private sector operator or supplier must bear and what the taxpayer will pay in recognition of *benefits which cannot be captured in cash*.[1]

I have italicised the words that broadcast the lie. Once again, we are informed that public investment in projects such as railway systems are "not profitable in aggregate". Reassuringly, the SRA informs taxpayers, who are expected to pay for the shortfall in finances, that Britain is no exception to the European rule that transportation does not generate sufficient profits to cover the capital investment and running costs of the service.

[1] Strategic Rail Authority, *A Strategic Agenda*, London, March 2001, p.24.

Mysteriously, however, there *are* certain benefits which do not surface in the balance sheets – but (asserts the SRA) *they cannot be captured in cash.*

Such a bare-faced lie ought to have left the SRA's readers reeling with astonishment; it is testimony to the propagandists that not a single economist wrote a letter to *The Times* to point out the financial error.

So how do I know that the Strategic Rail Authority is lying? Simple. I get richer with every passing day, because I capture some of those benefits. There is nothing ephemeral about the nature of those benefits. My bank manager does not turn them away. I deliver them to him once a month in the form of ready cash. And a lot of other people are doing the same thing. Yet, if you believe the SRA, this is just not possible.

Because of this chasm between the official myth, and economic reality, governments employ policies that are defective. This locks them into serious difficulties. Such was the case with the Blair government's attempt to formulate a transport policy. It walked straight into its own trap, and became embroiled in an unseemly public controversy just before the Prime Minister called a General Election for June 2001.

The economic doctrines that foster the lie are nurtured in HM Treasury. The government's economists know the truth, but for ideological reasons they remain silent. That is why the Treasury found itself embroiled in a damaging row with Ken Livingstone, the Mayor of London, and his Traffic Commissioner, Bob Kiley. The dispute was over the key features of a plan to upgrade London's Tube. An efficient service is vital, for 75% of central London's commuters use the underground and national rail services to travel to work.

According to Mr. Kiley, who is credited with modernising New York's dilapidated subway, the dispute could be attributed to the Treasury's dream. That dream was to find a way of shifting the cost of investment onto private investors under something it called a Private Public Partnership (PPP). Mr. Kiley, who warned that the Tube was close to being dangerous to the public's health, explained: "The Treasury had a dream at the beginning of this PPP having no exposure for the government. But of course, it's mostly not private money".[2]

The PPP was a sham; another linguistic technique for conning the

[2] Felicity Lawrence, "Tube verging on 'safety abyss'", *The Guardian*, March 26, 2001.

electorate. During negotiations between the Treasury and the Mayor's Transport for London, it was conceded that public subsidy to the tune of £1bn a year, on average, would be needed over the course of seven years. The legitimacy of that subsidy was taken for granted because, according to the Big Lie, the Tube could not by itself cover the costs of investment in a modern signalling system, comfortable carriages and safe tracks.

In fact, if you come with me as I walk the streets of London, I will prove that an efficient underground service *does* pay for itself, that all the benefits *can* be measured in cash, and that there is *no need* to shift any part of the cost on to the taxpayers.

Civilised societies need sophisticated transportation. If people are to achieve their personal ambitions, and enjoy the full benefits of modern society, they need access to integrated road and rail systems.

Paradoxically, for the last 150 years, mass transit systems have been persistently afflicted with financial crises. Either the roads and rail tracks are not up to scratch, or the carriages are obsolete, or the cars pollute us to death.

Crises with bus and rail transportation, and car congestion, are not due to inferior technological capability. Nor are they the result of a shortage of capacity to produce the most advanced systems for moving people between places where they live and work.

The fundamental cause of continuous under-performance must ultimately be attributable to government policies. *The responsibility has to be laid at the doors of politicians who refuse to adopt the one policy that would integrate all the complicated financial, technical and spatial challenges into one elegant solution.*

Tony Blair's New Labour strategy for transport offers an illuminating case study. HM Treasury, as advisor to the government, thought it had identified a Third Way strategy that harmonised the interests of profit seeking capitalists and public service delivering socialists. The government certainly needed improved policies, for it planned to spend £180 billion over the 10 years to 2010 on transport systems.[3] But, as I shall explain, this massive sum – a huge exercise in Keynesian pump

[3] Andrea Felstead, citing the Cullen Report, *Financial Times*, March 30, 2001.

priming – will not result in the diffusion of social benefits to people threatened with unemployment, as Keynes intended. The strategy rests heavily on the imagination of its Strategic Rail Authority, which was charged with the task of developing a "big vision" for the nation's railway network. The big-time winners will be me and my fellow landowners.

The public row between the Treasury and Mayor Livingstone over how to assign responsibility for running the capital's Tube strongly suggested that New Labour had not formulated the principles that would correctly delineate the interests that should be divided between the public and private sectors.

But when the dust finally settles over the financing and management of the Underground, we can be certain that one little detail will remain buried out of sight of the public: the efficiency with which the taxpayers' money is invested.

I claim that *the taxpayers who will be forced to hand over billions of pounds will be robbed of the major part of the income from their investment*. A relatively small number of people will benefit. They will be enriched beyond *your* wildest dreams. *Their* fortunes will fructify out of the investment by taxpayers; and still the capital will not have a financially sustainable transport system.

Public Private Partnerships was the name coined for the formula to finance public sector projects. The PPP was supposed to combine the resources of the two sectors to deliver improved results for everyone. The government needed a success. The chaos in the railway network, following the Hatfield rail crash in 2000, had badly dented the public's confidence in the hybrid system with which the government was experimenting.

The PPP model suffers from PP – the Piecemeal Philosophy that underpins the way we pay for public transport. Despite the injection of private capital and managerial expertise, passengers could not spot the improvements in the commuting conditions. Ultimately, it was a question of cash: there was just not enough of it to pay for public services. That is why, in March 2001

- The privatised Railtrack had to go cap-in-hand for money to the government, who coughed up £1.5 bn in bail-out money; and

- More than £900m in subsidies would be paid in 2001 by the Strategic Rail Authority, leaving only £400m to plan for the future expansion of Britain's rail network.

Despite the huge sums of the public's money going to support privatised companies, Mayor Livingstone and Bob Kiley complained that the government wanted to dilute the administrative authority of the agency that owned the Tube. Kiley wanted 51% of the ownership shares in public hands, to ensure a unified system of management. The government clung to its preferred model. Finance from public sources fell short, and the Treasury wanted to spend £13 billion on the underground network over a 15-year period, with money from three private consortia.

As the government battled with the Mayor, the *Financial Times* (February 19, 2001) – a champion of privatisation – urged the Prime Minister to yield in favour of the Kiley proposal.

The PPP would lead to a fragmentation of responsibility for the infrastructure and separation from the publicly-run train operator. The government clearly has not learned the lesson of rail privatisation. Writing 30-years contracts with the private sector which give the right incentives and provide for all eventualities is virtually impossible.

The PPP philosophy was fatally flawed even within the terms of conventional Treasury philosophy. Bob Kiley claimed that its implementation "would be unsafe and operationally inefficient". This was a serious charge of negligence to level against the Treasury, which fought hard for the contract it favoured. But that contract would parcel out 11 tube lines to three private infrastructure companies which, according to Kiley, would have little incentive or obligation to operate in a unified manner.[4]

The public was kept ignorant of some of the sensitive details that were uncovered by the Transport Commissioner and his team of negotiators, as they struggled with the civil servants. For example, the Treasury was

[4] Bob Kiley, "Going down the tube", *Daily Telegraph*, March 5, 2001.

promoting a model of privatisation that would reward the companies for crashing trains. How would this happen? Under the disputed contract a private consortium could lose its franchise without compensation if it was deemed to be inefficient. But if it lost its franchise because it crashed (say) three trains, it would have to be compensated for the loss of the franchise. The back-room boys at Mayor Livingstone's Transport for London, when they finally unpicked the significance of this provision on compensation, realised that this was a financial inducement to crash trains. It would pay a consortium that was in danger of losing its franchise to crash trains, so that shareholders would not suffer a financial loss!

But the arguments over the fine detail of the contract pale into insignificance against the real issue. I will prove that infrastructure projects such as the London Underground can be fully financed from private capital, if the gains to all beneficiaries are taken into account – not just those of the travelling public, for example, or their employers. In which case, Bob Kiley would be steering a unified Underground system fully privatised with neither John Prescott (Minister of the Environment) nor Gordon Brown (Chancellor of the Exchequer) as signalmen.

2024 Update

Looking back on this one year after the eventual opening of Crossrail, now named the Elizabeth Line, this chapter looks prophetic. And given the criticisms of the Crossrail project, the big lie is alive and well. As any report into the value uplift of Crossrail tells you, it's been massively successful already. The problem remains not that we are investing in transport projects that are loss-making but that the profits stay in the private sector. This gives us public investments and private profits.

One administrative change is that the SRA was abolished in December 2006. Its functions were split between the Dept of Transport, Network Rail and the Office of Rail Regulation. But the problems remain unchanged beneath the apparent "reorganisations."

Public satisfaction with the rail service climbed steadily from just over 70% to 80+% in 2020. Figures after the pandemic have been hard to collect. Service was obviously massively reduced during the pandemic and numbers are patchy after that especially as services have been cut and there have been rail strikes for the period 2022–23.

One source of discord with the UK rail service is when people campaign for improvements and the franchise operators blame the rail track company and the rail track company blames the franchise operators. This can go on for years before anything substantive happens. This is something Don foresaw back in 2001. One of the biggest challenges for competitive service is that there's no real way to introduce genuine competition to the railways.

One common complaint of UK rail is ticket prices. Almost any survey of train travel across Europe for day of travel fares (especially business fares) puts the UK at the top of the list (often tied with Norway). This becomes less negative if you look at prices for booking in advance such as saver and super saver tickets.

This BBC article from 2019 explains the situation in a relatively even-handed way.

https://www.bbc.co.uk/news/uk-49346642

If privatisation was such a competitive success, should we expect prices to be so expensive? And if the only affordable way to travel is to book weeks or months in advance, are we really encouraging people to use rail instead of road?

Chapter 2

The Gravy Train

I left New Zealand in 1962 and arrived in London with £200 in my pocket – enough to buy a suit from Burton's and live for a month, whilst I looked for work in Operational Research.

By 1965, after a year in the steel industry and a post grad. year at LSE, I had decided that the management problems I liked best were the super-large ones that needed the help of computers. I worked on transport and stock control projects for customers of LEO Computers such as Schweppes, Shell Mex, BP, and for the steel industry. Then, my employer, by now English Electric, began to market to the communists in Eastern Europe.

The opportunity to investigate the Soviet 1-year and 5-year planning systems was irresistible, and in 1968 I relocated to the tax-free "haven" of Moscow! In less than a year, with my Russian language improving as I analysed the data from their steel industry, I came to realise how easy it would be to sabotage the Soviet system. Computers in the ministries that operated the planning system were the certain way to harden the arteries of the communist economy, and permanently freeze out evolution in any sector run by the state. That belief has been borne out in the West, where the failures of computer systems have highlighted the ineptitude of British bureaucratic systems, which have multiplied and worsened the original imagined evils that state intervention was supposed to cure.

A notorious example is the Soviet-style intervention in UK farming by the Ministry of Agriculture. This has led to collective farm-scale disasters in the quality of food, health of animals (BSE and Foot and Mouth being markers of the bigger problem) and deterioration of soil, water and landscape. Backing up this interference in what should be a landscape of thousands of genuinely privately owned farms, are bureaucratic Kafkaesque computer systems, which, by tracking and measuring hundreds of inputs and outputs daily of everything from antibiotic shots to set aside fields, have reduced all but the bosses of the biggest *kolkhoz* farmers to the status and incomes of Soviet serfs.

In 1970, as embargo restrictions on high-tech exports to the Soviets were tightened, I argued that we could glue up the Soviet economy by shipping in thousands of big data processing computers!

My great plan was not implemented then, of course, but to my horror Whitehall began to nourish dozens of gigantic computer octopi. I began to realise that government intervention in the market economies was part of the problem.

I returned to London and in 1971 I bought a house near the new Victoria Line tube station in Pimlico. It cost me £15,000. I modernised it in my evenings, as I worked by day on computer projects. In 1977 I formed my own firm. Two years later I purchased a redundant electrical factory near London Bridge, the occupants of which had elected to "relocate out of London" – they went to Wales – with the aid of "incentives" from taxpayers. I continued to work with computers, but now it was the age of the mini-machines made by Hewlett Packard and DEC. But I was now getting my first exposure to the British commercial property market. My firm did not need all of the space, so I let some of it to firms that were also in the computer business. I was now a landlord.

Because we were located south of the river, I had to drag people by the scruff of the neck to view the offices and become my tenants. Rents were lower than what families paid for three-bed semi-detached houses in Hammersmith. I knew that landlords had poor reputations, but I was certainly not getting rich on my investment in property. What I put in my pocket, at the end of the week, I earned in exchange for my building skills.

As my company expanded, I came to regard my tenants more as customers. I bought and refurbished other buildings for our use, while continuing to work on industrial computer applications in Leningrad until 1991. Then the recession struck. Property prices crashed, and I began to buy additional buildings in the area. That was when I pulled out of computers. But it was hard work, and to retain my tenants – my customers – I lowered my rents by 25% during the four worst years of the 1990s.

Then you, the taxpayer, in 1993 decided to foot the bill for an extension to the Jubilee Line, with a station at London Bridge.

I found myself aboard a gravy train. In the autumn of 1995, I let 13,000 square feet and some vacant land to Costain Taylor Woodrow, the contractors for the Jubilee Line Extension London Bridge contract.

At first, for the minnows in the property market like me, the train barely moved. But large property firms that had no presence south of the river began to buy the grander vacant sites and empty buildings. Then, by late 1997, despite the fact that the new Tube line would not be opened for several years, I no longer had difficulty in attracting tenants from the West End and the City. This was when I began to understand how especially benevolent you taxpayers were to my property activities.

I first quantified the sums involved in my enrichment when I started to develop a 5,000 square foot site at 38–40 Southwark Street. There were two industrial sheds on the land which I knocked down. As my new building rose from the ground, it became obvious to me for the first time that neither the architects nor the civil engineers were making

The redundant electrical factory is now known as the Menier Chocolate Theatre. It's a much-loved part of London Bridge.

a killing (each had put in a competitive tender for the project), and it certainly was not the men who were drilling the pilings into the ground or the contractors who erected the six-story reinforced concrete frame who were getting rich.

So who was pocketing the windfall capital gains by sitting back and doing nothing? It did not take long to work out the answer. While wear and tear took its toll on bricks-and-mortar, which meant that buildings depreciated in value – and they had to be maintained for the benefit of tenants through investment of fresh labour and capital – the value of land appreciated by leaps and bounds.

It turned out to be yours truly who was making the killing.

The fortune did not come to me as the Head of Contracting on the site. That money was earned the hard way, as you could see from my hands that I worked with the teams who poured the concrete and placed the reinforcement.

It was in my role as the owner of the site that I boarded the gravy train as the government announced the route of the Jubilee Line. The nearest station was a walk of just three or four minutes from 38–40 Southwark Street. I had forecast a gross profit of 25%. Gradually, my expectations about the margin began to surge. On graph paper, you could say that my financial expectations could be tracked on an exponential curve.

Suddenly, I was being flooded with offers for this and my other properties. "Buildings" that had been out of favour for years were now prized assets (*see image, new building 38–40 Southwark Street*).

I was getting very popular without having to mix another load of concrete, but deep down in my heart I knew there was something wrong about this unexpected bonanza.

When I came from New Zealand, I worked on solutions to problems of how to improve management decision-making. The efficiency of firms had been improved by access to our computers, but even greater savings would have been possible through improved stock control and purchasing. The previous wastage was at the expense of the shareholders who invested their savings in these enterprises. They were entitled to a return on the earnings which they had saved and invested.

But here I was, suddenly reaping windfall gains *without having to save, invest or work* for the riches that were accumulating even before the first of the new sleek trains had begun to rumble along the tracks.

The original picture of 38–40 Southwark Street from the first edition. You can also see 34–36 next door that Don mentions in the next chapter. Don owned this briefly, losing money on the sale.

But I do not believe in manna from heaven. In the South Pacific, some islanders believe in riches dropping from the skies. Anthropologists call them cargo cults – they live for the day that riches would be delivered out of the heavens. But I can read a balance sheet, whether it is a firm's or a nation's – and no-one gets something for nothing, without someone else paying.

So I began to analyse how it was possible for me, as the owner of a number of properties in what had been a rundown area near London Bridge, to suddenly be the owner of properties that were being fought over.

If I was the beneficiary, somebody had to be the loser. The loser, dear taxpayer, is you.

The way in which taxpayers are ripped off is cleverly camouflaged by the use of esoteric language that baffles most sensible people. This works to the advantage of the Treasury. Because if voters are prevented from sitting in judgment on the bizarre techniques that are used to pay for public services, the people who make the decisions can escape the responsibility for poor performance.

Someone has to pay for an efficient train system and for the network

34–40 Southwark Street today. Notice the sympathetic development of 34–36 where two and a half floors were added. A top Chinese restaurant now occupies the ground floor. This is an excellently executed development that shows how density increases after transport projects.

of roads that criss-cross the country. Can we arrange a system of charges which are both fair and efficient? We can, but such a solution is alien to modern political philosophy.

A transport system involves two kinds of costs.

- The **capital cost** that has to be locked up in the infrastructure. This includes roads or rail tracks and stations.
- The **running costs** are incurred when trains are put on the tracks. Who should pay?

The visible source of revenue is the cost of the tickets that people buy before boarding a train. Broadly speaking, these pay for the running costs of the seats which passengers occupy. The price of a ticket ought not to be more than the small extra cost of providing a seat for the last passenger who boards the train (economists call this "marginal pricing"). The users of the trains could not be expected to pay for the capital costs out of the tickets they buy for their routine journeys. If capital costs were included in the price of tickets, many people would choose not to travel by public transport. Instead, they would take vehicles onto the roads, where they would add to congestion.

Is there another source of revenue out of which to pay for the "lumpy" investments? Traditionally, government underwrites these costs out of the general revenue which it receives from the public through taxation. So, for example, taxpayers who live in the North East of England contribute to the cost of the M25 ring road around London – even if they don't own a car and have no plans to drive down to London to enjoy the benefit of driving on the ring road.

This way of funding capital costs is not fair on the taxpayers who do not derive any benefit from the investment. Furthermore, raising revenue through taxation burdens the whole economy through the disincentives and distortions that are created by the conventional taxes which are promoted by the Treasury.

I came to realise that public services under the direction of traditional government policies failed to comply with the norms that rule within the private market.

Entrepreneurs are driven by various forces – market competition, the love of the products or services they deliver to customers, intellectual restlessness – to continuously search for improved ways of conducting their business. If the creative passions of an Edison or a Ford faltered, they would immediately be disciplined by others. So, the general tendency is to refine products, improve processes, cut costs – everything that makes it possible for ordinary folk, today, to fly by jumbo jets to the other side of the world for their vacations, or to furnish their homes with sophisticated electronic gadgets.

By contrast, governments persist with antediluvian ways that favour complexity rather than simplicity, inefficiency rather than cost-cutting.

And at the bottom of this anti-evolutionary process, I came to learn, was the tax system. Taxes shroud the market signals that would otherwise help people to be ever more efficient, ever more contented with their lives. Taxes, and the ensuing subsidies, and the arcane regulatory mechanisms that are supposed to compensate for "market failures", end up by distracting us all from the business of earning a living with the least possible amount of labour and material resources.

That is all very well, you will reply, but is there an alternative? The crucial question – the one that governments refuse to address – is this: is there an alternative source of revenue which could pay for public services and social infrastructure without inflicting negative influences on the economy?

There is such a source of finance. It is one that we all create, in our communities.

Unfortunately, the government fails to engage with the public in a democratic discourse on the fate of that revenue. This means that, as taxpayers, we are kept in ignorance, which is why we are routinely ripped off.

There is no mystery about where that cash could come from or the economic effects of treating it as public revenue.

Think about what happens when the government builds a new road to an area that was formerly very difficult to access. There is an economic boom as people move into the locality. I recall just such an experience. When I was a youngster, the north shore of Auckland was a ferry ride away. It was used for holiday homes. Then the taxpayers paid for a bridge to be built, and the north shore became New Zealand's largest city after Auckland City itself. Who pocketed the benefits of that public investment in a bridge? The taxpayers? No!

We have 200 years of experience to support the claim that the major beneficiaries are the people who own land in the locality. But the owners do nothing to improve their land to justify that increased value. Where, then, does that additional value come from? The increase in the value of land stems from the benefits that are produced by the investment in a new road or bridge. This process is known as capitalisation. After the costs of labour and capital have been met, the net benefits of new investment are captured by – or crystallised in – the land market. The increased productivity from a new road or railway, in other words, is capitalised into higher land prices. There is a solid body of academic literature that describes this process in technical terms.[1]

---

[1] A summary of this literature in relation to the capitalisation effects generated by investment in transport infrastructure is provided by M. Boarnet & A. Haughwout, *Do Highways Matter? Evidence and Implications of Highways' Influence on Metropolitan Development*, Brookings Institution Working Paper, 2000.

But why do those increased values go into the pockets of landowners? There is one reason only: the government fails to capture the whole of the value created by the public enterprise – the road or bridge – to pay for the costs of the investment. (For a case study of this effect, in relation to a school, *see Box 2:1*).

This is a dereliction of duty by government, which is supposed to deliver value-for-money to taxpayers.

Box 2:1
Homeowners enriched by good schools

When government invests taxpayers' money to improve the quality of schools, who pockets the net benefits from improvements in the standards of public education?

There is a premium attached to the best schools, and – despite the official claims that these cannot be measured in cash terms – this premium *can* be calculated. The value surfaces in the form of higher residential land prices, as Dennis Leech and Erick Campos from Warwick University discovered. Their case study was two schools in Coventry.

After deducting the influence of variations like the size and type of house, they discovered that *location* inside the catchment area of the desired school added 19% to the price of a house, in one case.

The researchers concluded: "Places at the schools can be obtained through the housing market by moving house, but … there is a financial cost of between £700 and £1,400 per year on average in the areas sampled in higher mortgage costs".[1]

If this additional value was captured by government – it was money that people were *willing to pay* – the schools could be financed directly out of the services provided to the families that benefited, and there would be no need to tax people who live outside the catchment areas. By failing to adopt this policy, however, government

- enriches the owners of residential land. They become the gatekeepers to the schools, and the price of admission is £1,400 a year; and
- penalises taxpayers – those whose children attend relatively inferior schools – by loading the extra costs onto them.

This inefficient and unfair outcome is not resolved by the New Labour Government's Cabinet Office Performance and Innovation Unit, which suggests increases in taxation of investment income and wealth, and higher rates of inheritance tax.[2]

[1] Will Woodward, "House price link to good schools", The Guardian, March 3, 2001.
[2] "Social Mobility", April 2001, London: Cabinet Office.

What would be the outcome if the captain of a private industry allowed part of the value created by his firm to be handed out in the streets to the casual passers by? He would be sacked. But this is the technique for ripping off taxpayers which has proceeded unchecked in Britain for 200 years, ever since William Pitt invented the income tax at the end of the 18th century.

We can now decode one of the key words used in discussions about the finance of public services: *subsidies*.

Politicians assume that public services cannot be self-financing. That is why they say that taxpayers have to step in with "subsidies". Those subsidies are huge in relation to public transport. But why can't well-patronised trains pay for themselves? In part, of course, they do: the running costs are covered by the price of the tickets paid by passengers.

The so-called subsidies are usually required to cover the capital costs. Why can't the rail system pay for its own infrastructure, if it is an economically viable service? The answer, it now becomes clear, is that they *could* do so, if they were allowed to retain the full value that they create. *That value includes the part which leaks out into the private sector and is capitalised into the value of land.*

How can that value be captured by the railways and used to cover the costs of capital investment? Rational finance requires politicians to fulfil their public duty. Government needs to use the tax system to capture the additional revenue created by a public service such as the rail system, so that the money can be used to pay for the capital investment.

This analysis, so far, exposes the notion of the *subsidy* as a word that is calculated to cover up the mismanagement of the British government. *If a rail network is commercially viable, it will pay for itself without going cap in hand to the taxpayer.* But under the direction of the Treasury, Britain fails to employ efficient practices. That is why Gordon Brown has no right to preach to Britain's European partners on the need to "subsidise" research and development on the continent (*see Box 2:2*).

This sounds as though I have identified a painless and fair solution to the problems of paying for improvements to the London Underground or the national rail network. The proposal that I shall describe is not the product of either socialism or what people understand by the word capitalism. But nor is it based on alien ideas. It has even been suggested as practical politics for Londoners (*see Box 2:3*). It is consistent with the principle that drives the markets for labour and capital, in which *people pay for the benefits that they receive.* That is Rule No. 1 in our private market economy, and there is no reason why it should not apply in the transport sector so that efficient metropolitan transport is fully delivered by private enterprise.

Box 2:2
Brown's Pot and the Kettles

H.M. Treasury has calculated that if Europe could match the US levels of productivity and employment, economic output would be 40% higher. This means that European labour, capital and land are seriously underperforming, even when compared with the serious under-performance that has been measured for the US economy.

Chancellor of the Exchequer Gordon Brown has embarked on a preaching mission within Europe, urging Britain's partners to match US spending on research and development. Mr. Brown's proposal is a "tax credit" which is presented by the Treasury as a *subsidy to private enterprise*.

Is Britain in a position to preach? Our

- output per worker is below the levels achieved in Germany and France. Similarly,
- output per hour is below the levels achieved in Germany and France.

Arguably, then, *the Germans and French ought to be preaching to Britain, since their total factor productivity is higher than ours!*

Reforms in Britain have failed to deliver the best results. Despite 20 years of market liberalisation, the UK has slipped from number 15 to number 17 in the rankings among advanced countries in *per capita* GDP. Productivity per employee and per hour are still 20–30% below Germany or France.

Despite the Thatcher privatisation programme and Gordon Brown's shift to stealth taxes, Britain continues to languish. Something has been missing from all the efforts to deregulate the UK economy. It appears that the public sector has not played its part. Professor Richard Freeman, Co-Director of the Centre for Economic Performance at the London School of Economics, notes (*The Observer*, March 11, 2001): "Anyone who uses UK public transport knows that it is a barrier to productivity. Most UK privatisations have improved economic performance. Rail privatisation has not. Re-think this one fast, Messrs. Blair and Brown. If the Tube becomes the next decade's Railtrack, we are all in big trouble".

Unfortunately, governments fail to apply the rule that people should pay for the benefits they receive, which is why taxpayers end up as the big-time losers (*see Box 2:4*). There is a historical reason for this, I know. The factory system of producing wealth was built on rules shaped by a Parliament dominated by landlords that prevented millions of people from earning the incomes that would enable them to pay for the services they want. That is why, in the 20th century, it was deemed necessary to introduce the Welfare State.

But now is the time to re-examine the foundations of the economy, to identify its fundamental flaws. And now is the historic opportunity to correct the weaknesses. The flaws and the solutions will emerge from my case study.

In Chapter 3, I describe the results of my investigation into the Jubilee effect on surrounding land values. In Chapter 4, I put my land value recycling model under the scrutiny of experts to see if it stacks up.

Box 2:3
Conservative Economics

Steven Norris was transport minister for London in John Major's Tory government in the early 1990s. He believed that efficient public transport was vital, and that the capital investment in new systems could – and ought to be – financed by the private sector. His insights grew out of his study of the Crossrail project, which would link the mainline stations at Paddington and Liverpool Street.

The renewal of the transport network was vital if London was to remain a leading centre of global finance. But who should pay? Norris reinforced the case for a new North London rail link by proposing that property owners ought to foot part of the bill. His revenue-raising policy was a windfall tax, which he promoted during the first London mayoral election in 2000. He was the Conservative Party's nominated candidate.

"The key to big projects like this is the enormous value it adds to surrounding property. Just look at the Jubilee Line Extension (JLE). That was part-funded by private contribution, most notably £400m from the Canary Wharf development owners. Property around that area where the JLE runs has risen in value significantly. The question is why did more businesses that benefit from the JLE not contribute to its cost?"*

* David Parsley, "City keen to revive plan for cross-London rail link", *The Sunday Times*, September 19, 1999.

Box 2:4
The Chunnel Free Riders

The casual way in which government rips off taxpayers is illustrated by the poor deal struck over the construction and financing of the Channel Tunnel Rail Link. This agreement was investigated by the National Audit Office (NAO). It discovered that the Department of the Environment, Transport and the Regions (DETR) had underwritten the cost of the risks which ought to have been transferred to the private company that was constructing the rail link with the continent.

But the important feature of the NAO's report was the acknowledgement that government concedes that a gap exists between what the users would pay and the benefits that are actually generated by the rail project.

The DETR attempted to estimate the value of the benefits that would accrue *"for which no market exists*, but which are judged to represent benefits to society"* (emphasis added). The automatic presumption is that the taxpayer is supposed to finance those additional benefits rather than placing the whole of the cost on people who directly benefit from the rail project. Disguised in the DETR's methodology is the reality – that what they call "non-user transport benefits" are the free riders who pocket large sums of cash by riding on the backs of taxpayers.

The closest the DETR came to acknowledging that landowners are bestowed with windfall gains is in the acknowledgement that the rail project would regenerate areas like Kings Cross in central London, Stratford, in East London, and Ebbsfleet in Kent. The department's Housing and Urban Economics Division estimated "The impact of the Link on development values in the main areas affected".* But they then calculated the regeneration benefits in terms of how much government would have to pay to create the number of jobs that would be created as a result of the investment. They estimated that the government's "willingness to pay" to create 50,000 jobs was £1 billion, which was then taken as the value of the benefits of the project which justified the investment in the first place. There was no public disclosure of the boom in land values around the stations which, because it was created by the rail link, ought to have been captured to finance the project in the first place.

It was not possible for the NAO to subject the DETR's value for money assessment to a full audit, because in at least two cases "The department was unable to locate the detailed calculations of the figure, so we have not been able to verify this [figure]".

* NAO, *The Channel Tunnel Rail Link*, London: Stationery Office, March 2001.

2024 Update

Don's experience of London Bridge before the JLE offers extraordinary views into a changing landscape – change that was turbo charged once the Jubilee Line was approved. All Don's buildings are still standing. The fundamental truth Don focuses on is as true today, if not more so – the return on successful public investments makes its way into increased land and property prices. Don's insistence that this should be collected for the taxpayer was not a socialist, interventionist idea. As he stated throughout the book, Don wanted the least government interference as possible. He staunchly believed that the private sector, in a market with appropriate incentives and disincentives, would always beat the public sector.

He was in favour of capturing the land gains for society not just because it was fairer for everyone, but that it was the only truly capitalist or entrepreneurial solution. Having more taxes on land value gains meant there could be lower income taxes so that people could keep more of what they earned from their work. You should not be punished for working hard through income taxes.

We have to change our society back to a genuinely entrepreneurial one where people are rewarded for their efforts. This starts with accepting that free riding is not capitalism. Being able to sit back and watch others create value for you is morally repugnant, even if you are currently seen as a "savvy businessperson" for riding on the backs of others.

Taxes should be fair, but we have a system where a basic rate taxpayer in the north of England pays for investments that benefit rich landowners in London.

All the examples Don cites for the effect of quality public sector resources stand up to scrutiny 20 years later. Whilst few people have copied the thoroughness of the Warwick University study of the impact of good schools on house prices, the UK Department of Education put the house price effect of an outstanding school between 8–15% nationally. A PWC study in 2018 put the premium at an average of £27000 for a good primary school.

https://www.pwc.co.uk/services/economics/insights/how-school-performance-affects-house-prices-england.html

Chapter 3

The Canary sings the Jubilee song

It is human nature to want to conceal one's good fortune from the clutches of the taxman. One way to do that is to claim that it is not possible to calculate the cash value that might be the target of the Treasury sleuths.

That is why landowners and their professional representatives do not challenge the claim that it is not possible to accurately measure rental income. If you look in the books produced by the Treasury, you won't find an estimate of the flow of income to the people who own the land of Britain! But we know exactly how much is earned by employees, of course!

Occasionally, this natural propensity to keep cards close to the chest creates a problem. Landowners realise that they would be enriched, if they persuade the government to channel taxpayers' money their way. But how do they justify that outrageous scam? The dilemma was neatly illustrated when Margaret Thatcher's government decided that it would patronise the development of the derelict docklands, in London's East End. Who was going to pay?

Docklands needed a railway. Plans were produced to create a light railway that would flow along tracks suspended in mid-air. How could the government – representing taxpayers – be persuaded to fund a railway that would increase the value of the land around the quays and along the Thames?

The light railway could be completely financed out of the increase in the rental incomes of those sites. But if the government had decided to fund the railway out of that rental income, it would have been at the expense of the land speculators who were competing for a slice of the capital gains! This dilemma required diplomacy and professionalism of the highest order.

Enter Nigel Broackes, one of the most distinguished property developers in postwar London. As Chairman of the London Docklands

Development Corporation, he wrote to the then Secretary of State for the Environment (Michael Heseltine) to justify the expenditure of £65 million of taxpayers' money on the rail system to connect the East End with the centre of London. He acknowledged that the public's money would raise land values. But Broackes was coy. *If the public could get a solid idea of how much it would enrich landowners, the issue might be turned into a political hot potato!*

Broackes claimed that the increase, "*though impossible to quantify*, will in my judgment be considerable, providing benefits to the Treasury on our own land and enhance land values generally to private owners".[1]

Why is it impossible to quantify? To find out – in retrospect – I turned detective to estimate how much money my fellow landowners and I had accumulated as a result of the generosity of taxpayers.

The Jubilee Line provided me with a case study. I wanted an assessment of the windfall to the owners of land, courtesy of the taxpayers' investment in the Jubilee Line along the south side of the Thames, which ended up in Docklands. I knew the area very well. It was here that I embarked on my career as an owner of commercial property. My tenants will tell you that I am a hands-on landlord. I rescued derelict buildings in the Southwark area south of London Bridge, so I have a 20 year record of values of sites around the Jubilee Line route.

A very interesting case is that of 34–36 Southwark Street, which is a corner site that I bought in 1992 after it had been gutted by fire. I paid £45,000. The timing was bad, for this was the year when the economy was in the trough of the last property cycle. I discovered that I could not incorporate the building into my new development at 38–40, so I offered it for sale. The market was dead, and I sold the site a year later at a loss – the new buyer paid £40,000. He, in turn, held it for 12 months and resold at an even greater loss – for £30,000. Nobody moved a brick on the shored-up building. Then, the market began to pick up after the Jubilee Line announcement. *That site was sold at auction in 1999 for £230,000* (see plate 2). Why was that property now so valuable? Like the Dome site it would have fetched double if the existing building could be pulled down (*see Box 3:3, page 26*).

---

[1] Cited in Fred Harrison, *The Power in the Land*, London: Shepheard-Walwyn, p.222.

The inaugural run of the first Jubilee Line train took place in Autumn 1999. The London Bridge station, 10 minutes' walk away, was opened for business – and the good times had arrived again, but this time with a vengeance! Landowners were all aboard the gravy train (*see Box 3:1*).

The Jubilee Line electrified more than the trains: it jump-started many new commercial opportunities up and down Borough High Street and Southwark Street. Ageing properties were renovated as owners felt the pulse of new life returning to the arteries of ancient side-streets around the old hop market.

- The power station a few yards from the Globe Theatre was converted (at a cost of £135m) into the Tate Modern gallery, offering works by artists like Picasso and Hockney. In February 2000 the government added a further £6m of taxpayers' money to the annual £19.8m subsidy to guarantee free admission for tourists, who were predicted to bring £50m a year into the surrounding area.[2]
- Warehouses beneath the arches of the overhead railway tracks were converted into chrome-plated wine bars that soon became fashionable.

Box 3:1
The gravy train

No. 57 Southwark Street, in the London borough of Southwark, was bought for £1m at the beginning of 1999. Less than a year later, in November, the land and building of 14,625 sq. ft. was offered for sale at £1.8m. But the owner's expectations were now upwardly mobile. In January 2000 the asking price was £2.3m – and No. 57 was sold. The real estate agent's sales literature left prospective buyers in no doubt about the virtues of the location: "It will benefit from the opening of the Jubilee Line extension which is likely to boost the already improving and exciting environment around this property" (KALMARs Commercial, Advertising literature, November 1999).

---

[2] Fiachra Gibbons, "Smith pledge on free entry to new Tate", *The Guardian*, February 9, 2000.

The £1m 57 Southwark Street in 2023. Whilst it's largely unchanged externally, it has been updated inside to create a modern office environment. The link below reveals the interior. Whilst general inflation has obviously been at work, it's still extraordinary to imagine buying a building for the price of a two-bed apartment today.

https://search.oneadv.co.uk/property/citybridge-house-57-southwark-street-london-se1-1ru/

The public's investment in the Jubilee Line was paying off – *for the owners of land near the stations* (See Box 3:2).

Box 3:2
The Bermondsey Badlands Turn Good

An empty site used as a car park went up for sale in 1997: 72–78 St. Thomas Street was in an "unsavoury" area of Bermondsey, and the new American administrator of Lord Howard de Walden's estate decided to get rid of it.

The asking price started at £400,000. There was some bidding, and the site was sold for £600,000. The new owners then bought an adjoining building for £500,000. All in, the property had cost £50 per square foot.

This was the market rate at the time, and the beneficiaries of the estate enjoyed their £600,000 when his Lordship died in July 1999. He bequeathed them with more than 120 acres of central London and a title that reached back to the Gunpowder Plot.

Then the Jubilee Line came on stream. And the late 9th Baron's piece of land quadrupled to about £230 per square foot. The Bermondsey Badlands had turned Good, but here was a slice of value that his Lordship's daughters and grandchildren would not inherit.

In the property market, anticipation of nearby public (or private) investment is of the essence.

The "Bermondsey Badlands 2023 edition. This site is still undeveloped and is now a semi-permanent pop-up called Vinegar Yard. It's open in the evening for food and entertainment.

This picture from the other end of the street gives you a clearer idea of the size of the land that remains undeveloped.

The arches under the line have been developed and are waiting for high end tenants. You can see its proximity to the action with the Shard at the end of the street.

Frankly, I was outraged at what I regarded as the insane economics of public investment. The burden of taxation on British industry was damaging the animal spirits of entrepreneurs; meanwhile, the owners of land could lounge about while getting rich out of the public purse. That was why I decided to investigate the scale of this bonanza.[3] I monitored the trends, walking the streets around the five new stations as they were being constructed in Waterloo, Southwark, London Bridge, Bermondsey and Canada Water. I conducted my private survey of the adjoining properties, plotted their use with a colour code on maps, and monitored the value of the sites. I gauged the response of land values to the prospect of the new mass transit system that would haul thousands of workers, residents and shoppers into the area. I wrote in my records: "I want to estimate the size of the gain around each new tube station along the Jubilee Line, to a distance of 1,000 yards". The unfolding story revealed an astonishing process of enrichment for the lucky owners of land.

First, I investigated all areas thoroughly within a 400-yard radius (4.5 million square feet) around each station. Drawing on valuations around my sites, and other properties, I made conservative estimates of the increases in land values. I was able to draw on local experience and the data that I had accumulated over the previous 20 years, as a result of my trades in properties. In addition, of course, I consulted the trade press, and discussed land values with other property owners and estate agents.

My analysis produced calculations that were straightforward and conservative. I established that the gains being achieved in the immediate vicinity of the stations averaged £100/sq. ft. This meant that the effect of the Jubilee Line announcement led to a gain of £450m.

Then I plotted another circle extending to an 800-yard radius, covering an additional 13.5m square feet. The increase in land value averaged £50/sq ft., yielding a gain of £675m. around the station hubs. Finally, I pushed the circle to a 1,000-yard radius. Not surprisingly, there was some falling away of values. I conservatively estimated the increases at £20/sq ft, yielding an additional gain of £200m. Adding up

---

[3] In New Zealand and Australia, I could have consulted public records of annual land values, since they are recorded by valuers separately from building values.

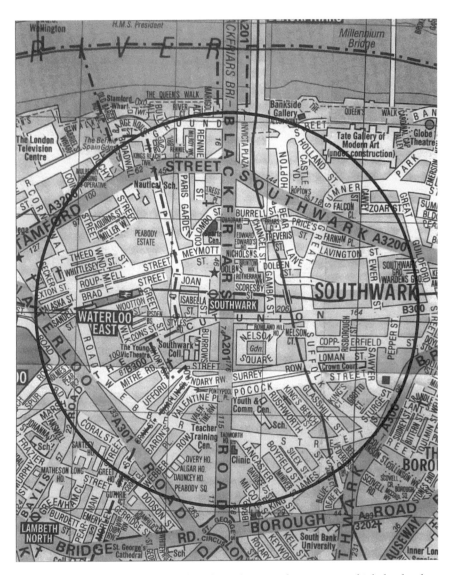

The 400-yard radius around Southwark Underground station in which land values were conservatively estimated to have increased by an average of £100/sq.ft. [Ed. This research has been copied by researchers all over the world. As far as we are aware, Don was the first person to do this.]

all these average values, the gain from the public's investment in the
Jubilee Line averaged £1.3 billion around each station.

I wrote in my records: "If the further five stations are included then
the 10 stations between Waterloo and Stratford have accumulated a
gain of around £13 billion, which is three times the £3.5 billion it took
to build the line"!!

Table 3:1
Major Classes of Owners Within 400 Yards of Five Jubilee Line Stations
(Waterloo, Southwark, London Bridge, Bermondsey and Canada Water):%

Public housing	30
Commercial property	19
Highways	14
Schools/Churches/Hospitals	6
Open space and Water	6
Retail	5
Private residential	4
Railtrack	4
Other	12

Railtrack itself was a major beneficiary of this explosion in values, as
was Southwark Council, which owned a large proportion of the land in
the catchment areas of the stations. Table 3:1 breaks down the
distribution of land uses on the basis of my estimates. The public sector
had a massive potential for drawing on revenue newly-created by the
Jubilee Line, if it moved fast to make the correct land-use decisions.

I was impressed by the magnitude of the increase in land values. It
seemed obvious that the Jubilee Line could have been constructed
without the aid of subsidies from taxpayers who live in the deprived
regions of Humberside and Merseyside.

I was particularly annoyed at the idea that the rich financial
institutions in the City – 20% of which are foreign owned – would
benefit from similar investment. The City was calling on the taxpayers,
to an important extent, to improve the transport infrastructure for their
benefit. Don't get me wrong: I want London to remain pre-eminent as a
global financial centre. But why should taxpayers subsidise their profits,
much of which would go abroad?

The new trains could be self-financing. The owners whose land
benefited from the Jubilee Line *would have been able to defray the cost
out of the value created by the Tube itself.*

My estimates of increases in land values provide an order-of-magnitude impression. A detailed survey would show values as a series of contours, from the peak around stations to the farthest periphery. The gradient would not be a smooth one, because each site is unique. Values vary within very short distances. A corner location can be worth more than the value of a site just a hundred feet down the street.

My project was disadvantaged by the absence of reliable data from official sources. People who are not informed about property values, therefore, might be tempted to criticise my estimates as exaggerating the total potential revenue.

- Many of the properties held by local authorities would not have sold for £200/sq ft. An example is Canada Water, which is located in the middle of the working class district of Rotherhithe. My street-by-street survey found that about 30% of the land was in public housing. Market values would be lower than the best prices achieved near, say, Canary Wharf or Waterloo.
- Compensating for this, however, the top £100/sq ft average increase under-estimated the values being achieved near, say, Waterloo Station. In the London Bridge area sites that were sold for £10/sq ft in 1980, when I first started to develop land, achieved levels above £250/sq foot.

So, my over-estimates for land in Rotherhithe are offset by underestimates for land further westwards along the Jubilee Line – and north-eastwards, where the trains dive below the Thames to transport people into Canary Wharf, where residential and commercial values have once again catapulted into a sky-high trajectory.

The Jubilee extension cost £3.5 billion and it delivered an increase in the capital value of land of the order of £13 billion. A 10% annual return on that £13 billion would yield £1.3 billion. A charge of 25% on that revenue would yield an annual flow of £325 million into the Exchequer, so the cost of the Jubilee could have been paid back over 20 years, while leaving ample rental income to fund other public services.[4]

---

[4] The rate of return on property varies according to the use. In a study of 1985 land values in Britain, 8% was the rate used for residential and commercial property, 12.5% for industrial property, and 5% for property in the public sector. Ronald Banks, *Costing the Earth*, London: Shepheard-Walwyn, 1989, p.39, Table 2:1.

Box 3:3
The Dome

The economics of public investment may be a mystery to politicians, but they are clearly understood by dealers in the property market. This is exquisitely illustrated by the Dome, which stands on the south side of the Thames opposite Canary Wharf. It was constructed on a derelict site at a cost of hundreds of millions of pounds to the taxpayers to celebrate the millennium.

The government invited proposals for its re-use after the Dome had served its symbolic purpose. New projects were proposed, but there was no doubt where the real value lay. According to the screaming headline on page seven of *The Independent* (Jan. 29, 2000): "Bidders for Dome 'more interested in the land' ". The hunt was on for the lucrative deals that could be spun out of the public's investment in the Jubilee Line. Readers of the article by Neil Mackwood in *The Times* (Jan. 29, 2000) were told that "The future routes to hot property" lay in investigating "plans for new transport lines before you buy".

Thanks to the Jubilee Line, the 48 acres site on which the Dome is located was boosted to one of the most valuable real estate properties in Britain with a selling price of up to £110 million. This valuation is double the sale price of the Dome in its use as a millennium icon. Property professionals announced that the government could make more than £50 million extra for the taxpayer if it abandoned the Dome in favour of uses for which people would be willing to pay much more – raising the price which builders were willing to offer for the site from £1 million an acre to between £1.5–2 million an acre if the site, given its close proximity to the Jubilee station, could be redeveloped.[1]

As the Blair government vacillated over how to dispose of the Dome, "government advisors believe the site can make £300 million if the Dome is levelled, [but] it is unlikely to rake in more than £160 million with the building in place".[2]

[1] Marie Woolf, "Tear down Dome 'to make £50 million' ", Daily Telegraph, 25, February, 2000.
[2] Nick Mathiason, "Ronson set to join race for the Dome", The Observer, March 25, 2001.

My assessment of the way in which taxpayers would have benefited from a new approach to public finance is a cautious one. It understates the actual prospects for funding services if taxation was re-based on the principle that the beneficiaries should pay for the services they receive. As a result of this, *a new synergy would explode in a virtuous circle of social renewal and economic growth.*

Public policy, as it is administered by the Treasury, is a major constraint on people's productive capacities. This is reflected in the increase or decrease in the economy's taxable capacity. The failings and strengths of government policy end up by either increasing or decreasing the value of land: windfalls and wipe-outs, and the scale of wins or losses depend on the location of the land.

The bible's original version of the Jubilee is a double event. Periodically, princes would cancel the debts incurred by people as a result of government policy (such as forcing people to pay for wars). The second act was to restore land to people who had lost it as a result of debts attributed to government policy. The modern Jubilee stood that philosophy on its head! *It deepens the public's debt, and it concentrates ownership of the prize sites.*

Government, in other words, defaults in its duty to ensure that taxpayers receive the full value for their money. If my findings are sound, the case appears to be made for a modernising government to at least test the proposition that public value is allowed to leak into private hands. Government must commission an official valuation of the land. The logic of such an exercise has already been conceded by government, which ordered the efficient use of all public assets. To this end, Whitehall undertook a valuation exercise that already answers some of the questions I have raised.

For example, should land used for public highways be included in the calculation of increased values? These tracts of land are not generally considered to be revenue earners, but this is one reason why so much public capital has been wasted. As part of the Blair modernisation project, the DETR shifted its appraisals from cash accounting to financial management. This entailed the valuation of highways such as Spaghetti Junction in Birmingham and the Hangar Lane gyratory in West London. Britain's first motorway, the M1 which runs from London to Manchester, was valued at £2.1 billion. The value of land, bridges and slip roads were included. An economist at the University of

Cambridge calculated that the rate of return on the Ml was more than 40% a year.[5]

It is not unreasonable, therefore, to require the best possible use of those assets under highways; and for the users of public assets such as roads to pay for the benefits which they receive. The Blair government recognised this principle with its White Paper, *A New Deal for Transport*, which includes the proposal to introduce road user-charges.[6]

Box 3:4
Canary bites the Taxpayers

The exquisite irony of our tax system surfaced in January 2000 when Canary Wharf, the property group that relied heavily on public transport to enrich its shareholders, trebled the rent payable by London Underground at its offices in the Docklands.

The Underground will have to pay £9 million a year – backdated to April 25, 1999 – on office space for which it had previously paid £2.88 million a year. This set the rent at £32 per square foot – in line with the rents charged by banks that set up business in the new 33 Canada Square building.*

Taxpayers who funded the Jubilee Line are now being thanked by Canary Wharf with having to pay market rents that public investment had done so much to increase.

* "Wharf trebles rent", *The Times*, January 7, 2000.

If the government ordered a valuation of land around the Jubilee stations, it would be assisted from April 2000 by the decision of the Land Registry to return to the practice of recording the sale price of properties. This provides an important database of market values.

Furthermore, the valuation exercise need not be limited to a snapshot of values on a given date. The mass appraisal of land values may have been a long and laborious process for William the Conqueror, who

---

[5] David Newbery, " 'Investment' earning Treasury 40 per cent a year", *Financial Times*, January 31, 2000.

[6] DETR Minister of State Keith Hill explained the government's philosophy on road usercharges in "Road-rents", *Land & Liberty*, Spring 2000, pp.4–5.

wanted the wealth of the nation in the 11th century to be recorded. But this exercise can now be executed rapidly and cheaply with the help of aerial mapping and computer power.[7]

There ought not to be controversy, therefore, about the size and distribution of value created by public investments. That there is controversy is a testament to the politicians' dereliction of duty. In defence of the feudal aristocracy, it can at least be argued that *they* were rational and open about their historic quest: to privatise the rents of agricultural land by taking power away from monarchs (using Parliament as their political vehicle). But in the era of democracy, the increase in the value of a vast range of natural resources, made possible by taxpayers, was privatised by default.

One result is an accounting system that leaves us uncertain about the costs and benefits that are generated by public investments. In the case of the Crossrail project between Paddington and Liverpool Street, for example, the estimated cost of construction ranged from

- £2.8bn (the number offered by London Underground's Crossrail project team: they are engaged daily in the economics of the rail network within London); rising to
- £4bn (Steve Norris, the former government minister who drew on the expert advice of officials from the Ministry of Transport); to between
- £6 bn and £8bn (estimate of the Corporation of London, the City's local government that could draw on the expertise of world-class financiers).

If the managers of private enterprises administered their businesses on the basis of such imprecision, shareholders would soon give them their marching orders![8]

---

[7] With the aid of these tools, communities can be empowered to participate in a new approach to planning the use of their environment and the chronicling of the land values that are the tax base. Denmark has long used committees of citizens to conduct surveys of land values in their communities for fiscal purposes. See Anders Muller and Gregers Morch-Lassen, "Land valuation and fiscal policy in Denmark", in Banks (1989), *op. cit.*

[8] The Blair government employed an estimated cost of £2.5 billion in its discussions within the Labour Party ranks on whether to issue public bonds to finance the Line.

It seems reasonable to conclude, then, that if the Blair government is serious about its modernisation project, it ought to implement a land valuation exercise as the first step towards reformulating public policy. The guiding principles would be the two equities – efficiency in the use of the equity provided by nature, and justice in the distribution of the benefits between the people who actually create equity value.

Some people might think that the beneficiary-pays principle in public finance is contrary to the principles of private property ownership. And yet, in that most capitalist of countries – the USA – we see an example of this financing as used in California. Since 1979, California's Supreme Court has upheld the use of what is called special benefit assessments, which local governments may employ to pay for infrastructural investments. Legally, a benefit assessment is not a "tax". It is a charge that can be levied to build a road, bury power pylons or, as in the case of Riverside, provide street lights.[9]

In Miami in the mid-1980s, part of the local funds for the Metromover came from landowners. The city created a benefit assessment district, which was the way of adding an annual charge to every square foot of downtown commercial space. Bonds were sold based on this revenue stream. The levy started at almost $0.20 per net leasable sq. ft., to decrease as more space was built.[10]

But this is an example of bitty policy when what we need is a general solution. A rational reform of taxation ought to provide a general and dynamic policy that rises to the challenge of free markets. What happens, for example, when some geographical areas experience a decline in the value of land? A new motorway can alter the commercial prospects of previously prosperous areas, which are now bypassed. Fiscal policy ought to be flexible and capable of a rapid response,

[9] "[T]he special assessment might be evolved into a tool to recapture windfalls from larger projects. Use has been authorized by judicial opinion for mass transit facilities and suggested for freeways. Enriched by concepts more fully developed in other chapters of this book, the special assessment may have a more expanded and glamorous future." Donald Hagman and Dean Misczynski, *Windfalls for Wipeouts: Land Value Capture and Compensation*, Chicago: American Society of Planning Officials, 1978, p.xxxv-xxxvi.

[10] *STS System Case Study; Miami Metromover*, July 1989. Trans.21, Boston, p. 5.

adjusting public charges downwards to ensure the viability of people who work and live in these areas.

2024 Update

As the introduction states, the TfL Land Value Capture report, including research by Savills and KPMG, effectively replicated Don's work in this chapter. That a single entrepreneur could be the first person to conduct this type of study is both amazing and concerning. That he has inspired others to do the same in what sounds like a more scientific manner is heartening.

The lesson is not to reduce government investments in major regeneration projects, but to invest even more, and ensure it increases land values. Wise investment makes a destination more attractive for people to live in. This causes land and property prices to go up. Much of this gain could be captured as tax, and other taxes can be reduced or eliminated.

Had the government bought much more land around the Dome at Greenwich, they would have been able to exploit all the gains that they were creating through their redevelopment of the area. This would have paid for the remediation work of the polluted land, paid for the build, and then the remaining profit could have gone elsewhere to Crossrail stations where the process could have been repeated.

If the government took this long-term investment approach with major capital projects, they would more quickly recoup their initial investment. This simple idea isn't implemented as any increased borrowing attracts criticism from landowner-run media organisations who accuse them of spending money on "white elephant investments". This means the gains of public investment continue to go to private landowners.

The Dome, once considered the whitest of white elephants, was renamed the O2 Arena and is now London's top entertainment venue. It's one of the most valuable assets for its owner, AEG, the sports conglomerate owned by billionaire Philip Anschutz.

For a business example of how a long-term view of redevelopment can work, one could consider Morrisons Supermarkets when they were still controlled by one of Britain's greatest retailers, Ken Morrison. Ken Morrison was as fiercely independent and entrepreneurial as Don. He considered finding land for new stores his greatest problem. Consequently, he was willing to buy much bigger sites than he needed for one supermarket in just the same way that Don would buy buildings that were too big for his staff.

Both men knew that the most difficult tenant to attract is the first one. Sometimes this "anchor tenant" had to be enticed with free periods, reduced build fees, and other incentives. But as landlord and tenant, Don and Ken knew their commitment to the site would attract others. For Morrison, his retail business became the anchor tenant. He then developed the whole site and leased and sold parts to other retailers or distributors. According to Morrison, his freehold properties were key to his successful retail business as it dramatically improved his cost structure. He was then able to compete with much bigger rivals. This strategy changed after he retired, and when Morrisons was bought by a private equity firm.

https://www.ft.com/content/26f606b6-09c1-11dc-93ae-000b5df10621

Chapter 4

Alchemy in the Land Market

Alchemists in the Middle Ages were convinced they could make gold out of base metals. They churned their stewing pots of chemicals, but never could discover the formula for getting rich without having to work. All the time, the formula was beneath their feet. There is one way only to get rich without having to sweat for it, and that is to let other people pay for the services that are delivered to the edge of your plot of land.

The something-for-nothing formula is not a secret. The brew is not chemical but political: it is to persuade taxpayers to finance public services, and rig the rules so that landowners do not have to bear the cost of the services from which they benefit.

Economists have also spelt out the formula for optimising wealth in society – get rid of the taxes that act as burdensome disincentives.

But there is an irony to the traditional opposition that landowners display towards the policy of paying for the capital costs of public services out of the rent of land. If they insisted on paying for roads, and for utilities such as water and railways, they would actually raise the rents received for the use of their land.

The algebraic proofs can be found in the specialist literature.[1] The conclusions offered here are from articles and speeches by Dr. William Vickrey, the Professor of Economics at Columbia University who was awarded the Nobel prize for economics in 1996 for the work which I am going to summarise.[2]

---

[1] William Vickrey, "The city as a firm", in *Economics of Public Services*, Martin Feldstein & Robert Inman (eds.), London: Macmillan, 1977. See also the study in the same volume by Professor Joseph Stiglitz, the former Chief Economist at the World Bank, who reaches similar conclusions to those of Dr. Vickrey.

[2] All quotations are from four chapters in *Land-Value Taxation*, Kenneth C. Wenzer (ed.), Armonk, New York: M.E.Sharpe/London: Shepheard-Walwyn, 1999. Professor Vickrey shared the Nobel honours with Professor James Mirrless of the University of Cambridge.

Analysing the impact of rent and the land market cannot be undertaken in isolation from what happens in the labour and capital markets, however. All three are integrated into a single system. In an open society in which people and their capital are free to move about, the returns to labour and capital are equalised throughout the economy. If we weld the private markets with the correct system of government finance, a surprising result emerges:

> Given the high mobility of capital and labour, which tends in the long run to equalize returns to these factors over the region, landlords ultimately reap most if not all of the benefit from an increase in the efficiency of the city, and should, if they fully realised their long-term advantage, enthusiastically support the change to land-value taxation.

Here we have the miracle of the land market. As science and technology forge ahead to improve the economy's productive capacity, so the net gains – after paying off the costs of labour and capital – end up in the form of increasing rents for the use of land. Dr. Vickrey spent a great deal of his time observing how people used public services such as the highways and he enjoyed writing algebraic proofs on the blackboard for his students to demonstrate the efficiency of treating rent as public revenue. Take, for example, the case of congestion. Public authorities are very inefficient in charging for the use of transport facilities that are in limited supply. Dr. Vickrey based his insights on his fieldwork observations, including the Woolwich ferry across the Thames which people used rather than going the long way round and under the Blackwall tunnel. He was particularly familiar with the horrendous gridlocks in Manhattan. What ought to be done? If congestion charges were imposed

> Speeds would be substantially increased over nearly all the day, air pollution would be decreased, and the locality would obtain a substantial amount of revenue. Businesses, especially the high-level ones, would be attracted by the improvement in the ability to circulate rapidly, property values would increase, and the yield of the land tax at given rates would increase.

Dr. Vickrey shrewdly spotted the parallel between the failure to charge for land-based public services, and the communist ethic. Noting the wisdom of restructuring taxation, he observed that

Automobile traffic involves the use of scarce land for the occupancy of which land rents should be collected and used to finance government. Present practices with respect to urban traffic are analogous to Soviet practices in which commodities are under-priced and shelves are empty and there is much wasteful queuing to be on hand when supplies arrive, which is much like driving around looking for a space about to be vacated.

Dr. Vickrey examined all the practical methods for charging for the use of public space, and he was confident that if parking charges were "properly calibrated, this would automatically keep the charges at close to the market-clearing level, enhance efficiency, and raise land values". But the beauty of this strategy is that it would enable government – without having to formulate a single bureaucratic rule – to raise the general efficiency of the economy. How?

Land taxes, congestion charges, and parking charges designed to promote the efficient use of the city's space should in most cases be capable of producing sufficient revenue to permit the elimination of most levies that impair its economic efficiency, such as occupancy taxes.

These new sources of revenue would be sufficient to cover the cost of providing public services, so that people who used the facilities – such as passengers on trains – need only pay the small cost involved in providing the extra seats required to carry people. Economists call these the "marginal social cost of each type of trip". I shall not offer a technical explanation for this use of the concept of marginal costs. The important point is Dr. Vickrey's conclusion that the public revenue out of rental income is crucial for supplementing the fares paid by passengers on trains, and "in the long run will result in the enhancement of pre-tax land rents by more than the required subsidy". In other words, as Dr. Vickrey stressed, it was in the landowner's interests to share the costs of public services by paying for the capital infrastructure.

Equity and efficiency are both served by having landlords contribute to the network costs of the services so as to enable their prices to be brought closer to marginal cost. In the long run the increased efficiency of the local economy would tend to redound to the benefit of the landlords by raising their market rents by more than the amount of the subsidy.

This is the modern alchemy (*see Box 4:1*)! And yet, for the last two centuries, landlords have conspired with governments to deny them the benefits of the formula for making themselves even richer!

If landlords in a community could be made aware of their long-run interests, they would voluntarily agree to tax themselves on a site-value basis to subsidize utility rates so as to permit them to be set at close to the efficient level, and find that the rental value of their land had risen by *more than the amount of the tax subsidy*. (Italics added)

After all, even my rough and ready survey around Jubilee Line stations in Chapter 3 had indicated that landowners reaped £4 for every £1 extorted from the taxpayers to build the Line. Likewise (*see Box 2:1, page 14*) if the existence of a good school enhanced property prices in the catchment area by 19%, homeowners in marginal areas could drive up values by getting together and investing in their local schools.

Box 4:1
Recycled Land Value

The advertisement in the *Evening Standard* on November 27, 2000, proclaimed:

FOR SALE BERMONDSEY 14,000 sq ft
Planning permission for offices
53–55 Tanner St
3/4 mile London Bridge Station
3/4 mile from Bermondsey Station
offers in excess of £1.5m

What this advert did not mention was that the new owner must pull down the existing building to realise the 14,000 sq ft, and that the land area is only 2,500 sq ft. Pre-Jubilee Line, the existing building and site might have fetched £250,000, i.e., £100/sq ft for the land with the refurbishable Victorian building thrown in for free. The asking price in 2000? £600/sq ft for the land!

Dr. Vickrey was more than a mathematician. He was also profoundly influenced by ethical considerations, which is why he also stressed that treating rent as public revenue was essential if working people were to share in the alchemy of the land market. For otherwise, competition in the economy would exclude them from a share of the benefits of increases in efficiency. For, as he noted, "landowners, as the owners of the principle non-movable asset . . . reap any gain from the improvement in the operation of the city or locality engendered by bringing utility prices closer to the efficient marginal cost level".

These principles of efficiency and public charges were not just anchored to the ground. They applied equally to the space above our heads. That was why "Airspace is a resource in fixed supply comparable to land and in principle commanding a socially generated scarcity rent. Airport landing fees should also reflect marginal social cost. Auctioning of landing and take-off slots differentiated by time of day and week is one possibility". The revenue from these rent-generating amenities would accumulate to enable governments to get rid of those taxes that cripple the economy while at the same time bringing order – and therefore greater efficiency – to the use of spatially-located public services.

Dr. Vickrey's testimony would have been important in helping Transport for London to settle its dispute with the government over the financing of the Tube. Tragically, the professor died just three days after the announcement that he had been awarded the Nobel prize. His friend and colleague at Columbia University, Dr. C. Lowell Harriss, wrote an obituary in *The Economic Journal*, in which he summarised the way in which the rent-sharing policy would finance urban policies.

> He showed, among other things, that a tax on land could facilitate desirable urban policies, i.e., taxes on an economic surplus, land rent, could help to pay for the fixed costs of public works, such as transit facilities, and thus commit marginal-cost pricing.[3]

---

[3] C. Lowell Harriss, "William Spencer Vickrey, 1914–1996: Nobel Laureate in Economics", *The Economic Journal*, 110, November 2000, p.F714.

But public finance was not just a technical issue, noted Harriss. The rent-based policy straddled the principles of economic efficiency with morality:

> In Vickrey's words: "Use of land rents, or, at least, of a major fraction of them, for public purposes is therefore not merely an ethical imperative, derived from categorization of these rents as an unearned income derived from private appropriation of publicly created values, but is, even more importantly, a fundamental requirement for economic efficiency"[4]

Dr Vickery saw that everybody gains, and most certainly the landlords. In New York City, for example, where the professor spent his working life, both the commuters and the owners of land would be better off.

> If the landlords of New York City knew what was good for them, they would vote enthusiastically for an added tax on site values to be devoted to lowering subway fares, especially for off-peak and shorter trips, and improving the frequency and quality of the service. Assuming that the subsidy would be used efficiently and not frittered away on administrative overheads, aborted, or put to grandiose construction projects or over generous fringe benefits, this would increase the value New Yorkers get for their outlays on subway service, increasing the attractiveness of the city, and in the long run raising site rents by more than the tax.

This healthy idea (*see Box 4:2*) ought to be the starting point for new negotiations between Mayor Livingstone and the Blair government for financing the London Underground. Bob Kiley made his reputation as the man who improved the New York Metro – but he could not achieve the best results that were technically possible because the metro does not operate on the basis of the best-practice principles identified by the Nobel laureate.

---

[4] *Ibid.*, p. F 715.

Box 4:2
A Healthy Idea

London Mayor Ken Livingstone plans to introduce road-rent charges. The revenue could be used to finance the money borrowed to pay for improvements to the Tube.

But rental charges are not only good for the economy. They are also good for people's health. If road charges are introduced, fewer wasted journeys are made, which reduces pollution.

- Between 12,000 and 24,000 premature deaths are directly related to poor air quality nationally and road traffic in London contributes 90% of its total pollution.*

* London Development Agency, *Draft Economic Development Strategy*, London, November 2000, p. 33.

But we need not rely on pure abstract theory for an understanding of how the landowner could – and should – contribute to new investment in public transport. Landowners are already demonstrating the wisdom of this policy. And to see how it would work on the basis of the empirical evidence, harnessing the mechanisms of the free market, we need not go outside the British Isles.

The Edinburgh loop

I advocate a reform of taxation which, from the viewpoint of Treasury orthodoxy, is pie-in-the-sky. How can we persuade the government and its civil servants to break new ground, and come up with sustainable public financing?

One way would be for the property industry to lobby for a change. It would be in the interests of property owners to promote the policy. After all, landowners would gain by sharing increased land values with the public.

Is this all theory? Not a bit of it. *This unique public-private partnership, grounded in the rent of land, is about to be tested in Scotland.* A group of hard-headed businessmen got together and decided that they could turn a 10 kilometre loop line that carries freight only around Edinburgh into a passenger-carrying network. Their plan is to pay for stations, signals and buildings out of the increase in the value of land along the line.

The total cost of this new passenger service is estimated at £32m. A company called E-rail was formed to make it happen. Property professionals and developers joined up with George Hazel, a civil engineer and Visiting Professor of Transport Policy at Robert Gordon University, Aberdeen. They identified 12 sites which, if developed, would enable the company to donate in the region of £15m into the pot to provide the passenger service. The other £11m could come from either of two sources:

- Planning permission to develop 60 more sites on which E-rail could have options from landowners; or, alternatively
- Edinburgh Council could make up the difference, by applying for a slice of the £150m allocated to Scotland's Public Transport Fund.

During the early stages of negotiations, the council indicated its willingness to bid for up to £25m from the Fund to invest in the new South Suburban Railway. But it has the power – as the planning authority – to make it possible for E-rail to provide the whole of the £32m, by granting planning permission to E-rail's other sites. That permission would boost the value of the land along the tracks and make it possible to fund the railway without a penny from the taxpayer!

E-rail was happy to proceed with the mixed ownership arrangement. So confident was it in the alchemy of the land market, that it offered to borrow the money from banks and provide the railway even before its sites were developed!

But I have to stress the really important point: *not a penny of public money need go into the capital cost of providing the railway* – if the council decided to fund the cost out of property development on as many of the 72 sites as it took to raise the cash. If that happened, Railtrack (which owns the line) and Scotrail (which would run the trains) would have a fully operational system without having to finance the infrastructure.

How would E-rail make a profit? Out of the homes, offices and shopping centres it would construct on its sites. In addition, it would receive its share of any profit that might flow from the £32m fund that was created to pay for the construction of the railway, if there was a profit to divide up among the partners.

All of this is what the theory of public finance predicts. And that is what the property developers and professionals in Edinburgh are willing to back by staking their money up-front. But the idea did not originate from algebraic equations. Instead, E-rail's John McGregor, a chartered surveyor, literally got on his bicycle and toured the areas on the south side of Edinburgh ... and wondered to himself: "What is all of this land doing here, vacant or under-used – and why isn't Railtrack doing anything with it?" And that was when the financing model hit him: pay for the developments out of the gains from a new railway.

- One project is to redevelop a small group of crumbling buildings which is called a "business park". E-rail agreed to purchase it for £500,000. "With planning permission, it would be worth £2.5m," says Mr. McGregor.
- But development can take place above the railway, as well. One project is the space above a deep cutting, in which E-rail plans to build 40 homes, each worth £250,000, and an 85 park-and-ride car park.

Will the trains roll on the Edinburgh tracks in 2004? There is one reason only why it should not happen: if the planning authorities drag their heels. But since the citizens of Edinburgh would be getting a new transport system that need not cost them a penny – as taxpayers – why should their elected representatives be obstructive? As Prof. Hazel puts it: "This is a win-win model of financing – everyone gains. The key to it is that E-rail forms a joint venture with Railtrack. We each put our land into the pool at current market value. Then, 100% of any uplift of land value goes to the rail project, and if anything is left over after the railway has been constructed, it can be proportioned out between us."

The across-the-board uplift in land values would be sufficient to encourage builders to risk their time and money to provide the citizens of Edinburgh with a modern transit system that would take people off congested roads and make the city economy more efficient.

The Edinburgh model of the public-private partnership can draw on some good precedents. In the United States, for example, studies have revealed that single family homes in the Boston area linked by commuter rail services enjoyed a 7% increase in properly value. In Philadelphia, residential properties were found to have rent premiums of 4% to 10% for properties near the region's commuter rail stations.[5] Research has also revealed a similar effect in commercial property values in Atlanta, where offices commanded rents of $2 to $5 per square foot more than similar offices a few blocks away from stations.

In the suburb of Lilyfield in Sydney, in anticipation of a light rail system (trams), which opened in August 2000, prices began to rise four years before. Jeremy Martin, a local property sales manager, noted: "Every time an article came out in a paper about the light rail, or the government said anything about it, we'd get a surge of interest". Prices of property rose by more than 50% since 1996. The Lilyfield link, built on disused freight lines, cost only A$20m.[6]

Is there any reason why the Government in London should not tap into such increases in land values and yields to pay for more of the services that the public wants?

2024 Update

Nothing happened to the Edinburgh Loop. All the ideas in this chapter failed to gain sufficient support and so the line remains in similar use as 20 years ago.

One thing that did change was Tanner Street, London. It's a fantastic example of what happens to high quality, old housing stock when you dramatically improve the transport links.

As Don said, 53–57 Tanner Street had an asking price of offers over £1.5m in 2001. This site remained unsold for years but was eventually purchased by a housing association, London and Quadrant (L&Q). They bought the building next door and created a plan to put 154 apartments on the enlarged site. The plan was controversial as it

[5] Robert Armstrong, "Impacts of commuter rail service as reflected in single-family residential property values," *Transportation Research Record*, Transportation Research Board, Washington, DC: National Academy Press, 1995; and Richard Voith, "Transportation, Sorting and House values", *AREUEA Journal*, Vol. 19, No. 2.
[6] Jennifer Stynes, "All stops to Lilyfield", *Sydney Morning Herald*, August 19, 2000.

The original area looked like 45–47 Tanner Street (this sold for £10m in 2016).

This is the apartment building today. In 2023, a single two-bed apartment in the block sells for £900–950k.

https://nethouseprices.com/house-prices/53%20Tanner%20Street,%20London, %20Se1?page=1

demanded a massive increase in housing density in the area. The first application was rejected, followed by a public inquiry, followed by an appeal where it was approved.

https://www.london-se1.co.uk/news/view/4205
https://www.london-se1.co.uk/news/view/4664
https://www.london-se1.co.uk/news/view/4849
https://www.lqgroup.org.uk/

Tanner Street itself may be one of the best examples of how an area is developed as transport links are improved. Beginning at No.1 Tanner Street, it is evident that the area has been beautified. At the end of the street, and up to 61 Tanner Street, the old, restored buildings give way to higher and higher new builds.

The neighbour to this newer development is a leading budget hotel chain. They too are pushing the height limits on the site and building higher and higher to maximise the return on the site.

The images reveal that the original building with 4 floors now has 8–10. At the time of publication, the budget hotel group is further increasing their building of 10 plus floors.

The view from No.1 Tanner Street at the Bermondsey Road end.

In late 2023, a budget hotel chain is building even higher showing how once you move above the historic building height, things tend to go even higher.

Tanner Street is worth an exploratory walk. It's like walking through a time tunnel of development from sympathetic restoration to new buildings reaching for the sky.

Chapter 5

Subways and the Free-riders

The fate of the 21st century will be determined in the great metropolitan centres of the five continents. Mega-urban sprawls will soak up the misery of landless peasants who will be the festering sores on the global economy.

The conurbations that flourish will need the best forms of mass transit that the computer age can devise. But *we know that these new systems will bring painful problems even to the advanced countries if they are not linked to the correct methods for financing both the capital infrastructure and the back-up social services.* Two examples of how the benefits can be distributed expose the weaknesses of conventional government thinking – and, in the case of Hong Kong, the enlightened way in which to combine commercial sense with sound social strategies.

Washington DC

In 1980, the Senate approved a $24.8 billion Federal subsidy programme for US mass transit systems. The money was to be spent during the following five years.

The Metro planned for Washington DC was described by *Fortune* magazine as "the solid-gold Cadillac of mass transit".[1] The cost was originally put at $2.5 billion. But from the day of the first groundbreaking, in 1969, taxpayers were informed that the cost would escalate to $7.2 billion. Of this, 80% would come out of Federal funds. By 1980, taxpayers in the backwoods of the United States who had nothing more than a dirt track leading to their doors would subsidise the air-sprung comfort of people who worked within short distances of Capitol Hill.

---

[1] H. Nickel, "Washington's Metro is the solid-gold Cadillac of mass transit", *Fortune*, December 3, 1979.

Taxpayers footed the bill, but who pocketed the net value – the income that is left after paying for the labour and capital costs of constructing the Metro? A congressional staff survey revealed that land values around Metro stations had increased by $2 billion in the five years since the first train glided out of Farragut North in 1975.[2] This calculation was based on conservative assumptions. Real estate experts in Washington said at the time that the correct figure was more like $3.5 billion.

Three studies examined the growth of population and employment in the Washington, DC, areas to measure the influence of rail stations. They found that areas with access to the Metro grew more quickly than areas that lacked this access.[3]

Walt Rybeck, Director of the Center for Public Dialogue and one of Washington DC's experts on land economics, has monitored the economic impact of the capital's subway system for the past 25 years. As special assistant to the late Congressman Henry Reuss (who at the time was Chairman of the House Committee on Banking, Finance and Urban Affairs), Rybeck authored a study on the impact of the Metro on land values. Metro opened in 1976 and was 40% complete at the time of the research. Looking back on that experience, he now reports:

In 1981, with some $3 billion in expenditures toward building the system, we conservatively measured over $2 billion in new land values that would not have existed without the subway. The originally planned 103-mile system was completed January 2001 at a total cost of $9.5 billion. It is safe to estimate that between $10 billion and $15 billion in new land values have been generated to date [March 2001] by this major infrastructure serving the nation's capital area.

Metro is popular with commuters and visitors, but it suffers from free riders – the adjacent property owners who may not ride the trains but who get huge windfalls from this public investment. The *Washington Post* typically includes a dozen ads by estate agents and businesses capitalizing on their Metro benefits. Examples: "Adjacent to Van Ness

[2] L. M. Simons, "Value of land around Metro leaps dramatically in five years", *The Washington Post,* January 24, 1981.
[3] Transit Co-operative Research Program, *TCRP Report 16: Transit and Urban Form,* Transportation Research Board, Washington DC: National Academy Press, 1996, p.28.

Metro stop." "Just 1 ½ blocks from Metro." "Easy walk from Rosslyn Metro exit."

> While private owners pocket the lion's share of Metro-created land values, Metro cries that it is running short of funds for maintenance, operation and line extensions the public wants. Potent environmental groups – the Sierra Club, Friends of the Earth and the Washington Regional Network – urge officials in the region to recapture the land values created by Metro. A land tax to support Metro, they say, would suppress land speculation along the routes, foster development in existing urban sectors, and stem the sprawl that is invading farms and scenic areas surrounding Washington.[4]

The outcome of the need for a modernised underground system in the capital of the US, then, was a financial burden on people who earned their wages. But it was a staggering windfall gain for the people who owned land that was strategically located around the Metro stations.

Was this a financially sane way to pay for a public project? Taxpayers suffered a double whammy.

- They paid for the construction of the Metro which other people would use.
- They suffered the disincentives of a tax burden that reduced the income they would otherwise have been willing and able to produce.

Was this a morally sound basis for distributing the benefits of the capital investment?

- Taxpayers were robbed of their incomes for someone else's benefit.
- Society suffered: some people, priced out of jobs because of the added costs on employers of having to pay taxes, were driven by necessity to behave illegally – such as dodging the taxman. This is not the way in which public policy should encourage people to behave.

---

[4] Personal communication, March 28, 2001.

Is there a more sensible way to build and run a railway? The British colony of Hong Kong developed a model from which the rest of the world could learn.

Hong Kong

We saw (Chapter 4) that distinguished economists like Dr. Vickrey identified a sophisticated partnership for both finance and management of mass transit systems. He recommended that the capital costs should be underwritten out of the increases that they generate in the value of land.

If this is a practical proposal, it means that public transport can be both self-financing and ethically fair to everyone.

If this policy were practical, it would also pass one of the tests of the environmental movement – a sustainable arrangement. For as the transport system expanded, so it paid for its capital costs out of the ever-increasing value of the land which fell within its catchment area. And passengers would pay for no more than the additional costs of providing the seats on which people wished to place their bums while commuting to work.

The experts in Britain examined this model as a result of the need for further modernisation of the British Rail network. The earlier electrification had raised land values.

There is evidence that this has occurred with previous electrification schemes, but it has not been possible to assess the magnitude of the effect which might arise from a large electrification programme.[5]

According to the evidence gathered by the government investigation, there was a problem with monitoring the increase in land values.[6] Civil servants may have thought there was a problem, but property market specialists knew exactly how to calculate and track changes in the value of land. *That is why they buy land near stations – preferably before the planners and rail builders announce their plans!*

---

[5] Department of Transport/British Railways Board, *Review of Main Line Electrification, Final Report* London: HMSO, 1981, p.76, para. 42.
[6] *Ibid.*, p.77, para 43.

Property professionals around the world are constantly tracking the price of land in the market place. And government agencies from Denmark to New Zealand make it their business to assess land values for the purpose of recovering part of the rental income of land for the benefit of the people who create it – the taxpayers.

So when the British colonial government in Hong Kong decided to extend the Island Line, it had no doubt how best to finance the project.

In 1980 it estimated that the cost would be HK$7 billion. Unlike the Federal government of the United States, however, the Hong Kong government decided that the capital costs should be paid for by the people who gained from the construction of stations along the new line.

Of the total cost, HK$5 billion was to be raised through the profits that would be reaped from property development around the 13 underground stations. This model of financing did not escape criticism. One commentator said that it was "bizarre". The Chairman of the Mass Transit Railway Corporation hit back in these terms:

> I would have preferred the description to be progressive or realistic ... World experience as well as that in Hong Kong indicates that property values in the vicinity of newly opened underground railway stations tend to increase dramatically. By allowing the corporation to develop the air space above stations and depots, the government has diverted a portion of the profits arising from such an increase in property values towards the financing of the railway. What is bizarre about that?[7]

This model of public finance and investment recognises two things:

- Equity is created in land which the community captures to finance the costs of the improvements.
- There are no losers. Everyone gains through their access to the transport system (*see Box 5:1*). And anyone wanting a windfall fortune is free to gamble his money on a lottery ticket.

[7] N. S. Thompson, "Tunnel vision on the MTR", *Far Eastern Economic Review*, January 30, 1981.

Box 5:1
The Hong Kong way with rails

Hong Kong is a hilly outcrop. Its rail tracks cling to difficult terrain which makes the cost of construction expensive. Even so, unlike rail networks in other countries, the Hong Kong system receives no public subsidies.

Since the 1970s, Hong Kong has completed a network of 143 kilometres. About 55% of the population is now within walking distance of the rail stations. The network carries 3.5 million passenger trips every day, which is more than 30% of total public transport use.

The government is working towards the completion of six new railways between 2002 and 2005, costing more than HK$110billion.

With the population forecast to grow from 6.5 million to almost 9 million in 2016, cost-efficiency in a land-scarce territory is vital. When completed, the network will stretch 250 km., and more than 80% of the population will fall within the rail catchment.

Although the government undertakes the strategic planning, the railways are operated by two public corporations which continue to operate at a profit. The government has announced plans to partially privatise the Mass Transit Railway Corporation to provide "an alternative source of financing and [to] reinforce the commercial principles under which the Corporation has operated successfully", according to Secretary of Transport Nicholas Ng.

London will receive a grant of £3.2bn. over the years to 2004 from the Treasury. This subsidy for transportation excludes money for the underground, on the assumption that the tube should break even (which everyone knows it won't).

Bob Kiley, who was imported to London by the Mayor because of his record in New York, says that the Underground should be part financed by £4.4bn loans from the bonds market. These, in turn, might be partly financed out of congestion charges revenue, estimated at £180–190 million – road rents paying part of the cost of the underground network. The link with road rents is still being discussed at Transport for London as a policy target for 2003.

The cost of financing the bonds is a contentious issue, and Bob Kiley claims that more transparency is needed from the Treasury, which he accuses of cooking the books to promote its version of the PPP (*see Box 5:2*).

But is it reasonable that part of the cost should fall on taxpayers? Look at the New York experience.

The New York subway improvements were paid for largely out of bonds that were floated on the capital markets, and out of general taxation (*see Figure 5:1 on page 48*). But why should US citizens who live outside the Big Apple – like New Mexican immigrants struggling to make a living on the margin of subsistence – help to pay for a subway that enriches New Yorkers? The evidence that investment in mass transit infrastructure *does* pay for itself is everywhere to be seen.

An example of how a road creates a stream of rental value in perpetuity is a nine-mile stretch of I-87, a section of the New York State Interstate Highway known as The Northway. This was constructed in the late 1950s. Right of way and construction costs were in the range of $128 million (in current dollars). The additional land value generated within two miles on either side has totalled $3.734 billion, according to Dr. H. William Batt, Executive Director of the Centre Research Group of Albany, New York.

Box 5:2
Cooking the Books

London Transport Commissioner Bob Kiley claims that the Treasury "cooked the books" to justify pressing ahead with the award of contracts to four consortia which would assume responsibility for the underground infrastructure for 30 years.

London Transport's simulation model (formulated by a US consulting firm with ties to Massachusetts Institute of Technology) compared the performance of each private bidder, and found that the private deals failed to match the benefits of keeping the underground in the public sector. But the Treasury rigged the results. It employed a wheeze not familiar to respectable economists.

Mr. Kiley revealed: "Recently I have found the underground and its consultants saying that, while public sector borrowing costs would be substantially cheaper, a bizarre Treasury theory ("reputational externalities") not recognised by any responsible economist or financial expert could offset most of these savings".

Mr. Kiley did not object to private consortia working with the underground to improve the service. But he did object to the fact that "the government has spent three years and £100 million in consulting fees to lawyers and accountants. If they sign the contracts, they will commit taxpayers to subsidising private companies with upwards of £1 billion per year for 30 years".*

*Bob Kiley, "I am losing my battle to save the Tube", *The Guardian*, May 2, 2001.

Figure 5:1 New York subway finance (1995–99)%

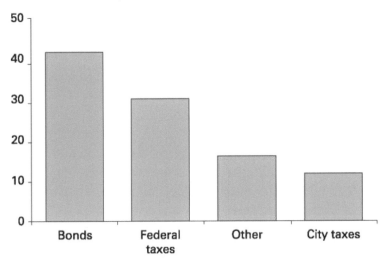

Source: Stephen Glaister and Tony Travers, "Bonds for beginners", *The Guardian*, March 20, 2001.

According to Dr. Batt, "the capital finance of the Northway, at least in this area, could easily have been done by recapturing these windfall gains that fall to private landowners. One could argue that this added value, the direct result of public investment, should rightfully be returned to the public and should be recaptured to pay off the bonds that were issued to build the project, rather than left for opportunistic speculators to reap private gain".[8]

But while taxpayers create value, their governments, as we shall now see, are busy destroying value.

[8] H. William Batt, "Value capture as a policy tool in transportation economics", *The American J. of Econ. & Sociology*, Vol. 60 (1), January 2001, p.196.

2024 Update

Instead of offering updates on the overseas examples Don cites, it's more relevant to consider the impact that Crossrail has had on London and surrounding areas in the last 10 years or so.

One of the claims of the opponents of changing the tax system is that the uplift that comes from the development of a new or improved station or transport link cannot be calculated. Given Don's work and subsequent work by TfL, Savills, KPMG, and other groups around the world, this claim is nonsense.

Additionally, property agents in the UK have been monitoring the uplift of land values throughout the planning, building, and opening of the Crossrail project. Again, they show the exact same thing: massive increased in land and property values. Criticism of this book could be "That was 20 years ago." and that the criticism of TfL could be, "Well, you're TfL, you're bound to say that!" Let's take a look at the impact that Crossrail has already had on land and property values.

The following studies provide competitive data from property agents seeking to attract investors to buy property and land from them. The agents knew Crossrail would increase the value of land around a new or improved station, so they used their expertise to attract long term, profitable clients who can purchase several properties at once, e.g., an entire floor of a new apartment block. Whilst short term points are gained for exaggerating potential gains from a new station, they are lost very quickly with professional investors who then take their business elsewhere.

The first study is from the JLL research team. JLL is one of the world's top property agents. This research was completed by their London team, headed by researcher Meg Eglington. The following were their conclusions.

- *Growth in average prices in areas surrounding 76% of Crossrail stations outperformed the regional average.*
- *18 stations have experienced sales price growth of over 70% since 2012.*
- *Largest premiums typically found along the Eastern lines. The biggest increases were positively correlated with the largest time savings to get into Central London.*

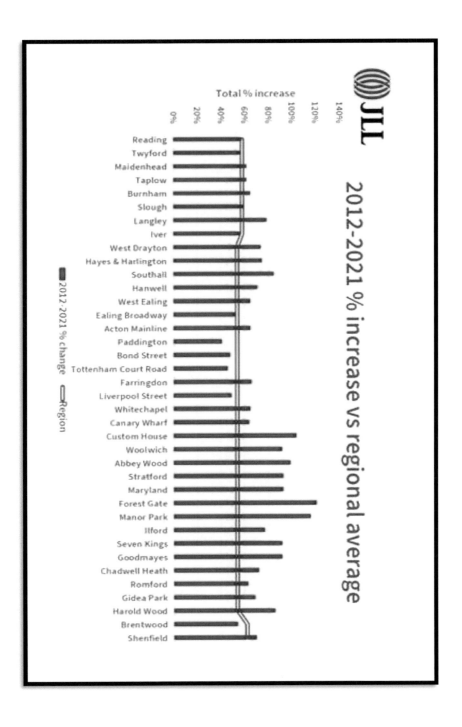

https://residential.jll.co.uk/insights/news/crossrail-may-2022

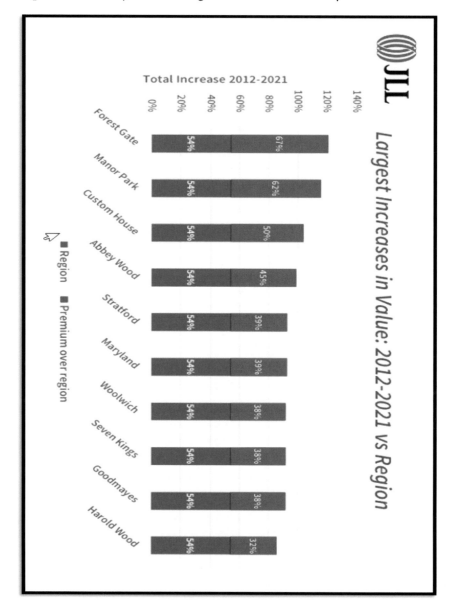

- *Younger people tend to be moving to the East from central areas to get better value accommodation and families are now moving west for larger family homes.*
- *Areas that were already well connected, especially the central area, were much less affected as there was little or no improvement.*

The JLL research captures perfectly the uplift before the line opened in May 2022. In summary, developers and homeowners moved into the area as the build was progressing to take advantage of lower prices and the anticipated uplift.

Interestingly, since opening, there has been something of a retrenchment in prices. As this has coincided with an increase in interest rates between 2022–23, we need to look at the controls to filter out the Crossrail effect. Another agent in London, Benham and Reeves, has been tracking prices and their most recent research shows that 20 Crossrail stations have seen lower growth than the surrounding areas since the line opened.

On average, across the line, prices climbed by +2.4% v 19% for the wider local authorities.

Of the best performing stations, Forest Hill continues to race ahead. In the Newham borough, there were price increases of 9% near the station, compared with a small decline of -0.1% for the wider area. However, the best performing station was Romford, an area that had lagged behind other stations on the line until the opening (as seen in the JLL research). Romford prices increased by 14% compared with 4.4% for the wider Havering area. The perception here is that more families are drawn to Romford than other areas, and they are more likely to wait for the station to open before making a purchase.

What is also interesting is that both Liverpool Street and Bond Street have seen double digit growth compared to their local controls. The other top 10 Crossrail stations to have posted a stronger performance when compared to the wider area in which they are located include Brentwood (+5.8%), West Drayton (+5.8%), West Ealing (+4%) and Hanwell (+3%).

One local drop was Canary Wharf, which fell by -17% 2022–23. This has been attributed to the announcement by HSBC that it is moving its headquarters to central London. Given the relatively low number of people directly affected by this, this decision has been interpreted as a precursor for more large firms to leave Canary Wharf. Consequently, the estate owner is working to increase the desirability of the area as a place to live and not just a place to work.

Property values surrounding no less than 18 other Crossrail stations have also underperformed when compared to their wider local authorities: – Gidea Park, Acton Main Line, Southall, Woolwich, Custom House, Twyford, Reading, Tottenham Court Road, Stratford, Maryland, Langley, Abbey Wood, Slough, Burnham, Goodmayes, Seven Kings, Manor Park, and Harold Wood. If you are interested in this research, please see the link below:

https://www.benhams.com/press-release/london-property-market/ have-london-homebuyers-ended-their-crossrail-love-affair-already/

In spite of the short-term fall, Benham and Reeves director, Marc von Grundherr, commented:

"It's fair to say that since launch the shine has perhaps faded across many pockets of the network now … [However] … We are currently seeing very strong demand for rental homes within the Whitechapel area and it currently ranks as one of our top five rental hotspots across the city. As a result, rental values are climbing and this is providing some extremely favourable yields."

This is consistent with unpublished research from JLL that has been monitoring rental yields across the line and they are reporting extremely high increases in rental yields in 2023.

Why are there such large differences in land value increases and are there ways of predicting in advance the scale of the uplift? The TfL study helped to clarify this (along with Don's own research). Simply, a new or improved station is not enough. It has to be accompanied by additional elements. To focus on the biggest increases, first, look for the travel time saving. Then look at where the time gain allows you to travel; specifically, does it allow you to travel to areas of high paying, desirable work? The biggest increases focus on locations that save commuters travel time, including areas in which the time saved allows the commuters access to higher paying, more desirable work locations.

The transport project that fails Don's *"Does it increase land values?"* test transports people from one poor area to another. The trains need to transport people to increased opportunity. London Bridge benefitted so much in part because commuters could travel quickly to the docklands, a place where high paying jobs were plentiful. And in the last 20 years there has been massive investment in and around the waterfront at London Bridge attracting high paying jobs to London Bridge itself.

Well-meaning but misguided politicians can promote transport projects that link areas of poverty. Sadly, this helps no one unless it is linked with massive regeneration projects. It's much better to link poor areas to affluent ones.

The largest land value increases also depend on its adjacency to another prosperous area. This allows people who can't afford the most prestigious postcode to live close enough to enjoy the benefits of the more desirable area without having to pay for the privilege. And residents of the nicer area are enticed to move there themselves to take advantage of higher value housing.

If an area is less desirable and consequently has a higher potential benefit from the transport improvement, there must be plans to improve other infrastructure such as schools, healthcare, and leisure amenities.

In the last cycle, investors looked for what became known as the "Café Rouge effect". Café Rouge is a mid-range restaurant chain offering French inspired dishes. They had a habit of moving into an area as incomes increased. So, if a company can't conduct their own socio-economic research, they could look for an intelligent management team of a larger, successful business to do it for them. Another factor that can lead to rising land prices is older housing stock. This was prevalent along the Jubilee Line. Older housing stock offers two opportunities for developers: renovate to create highly desirable, expensive accommodation, or demolition, and rebuild with increased density and quality. This improvement in housing stock attracts higher income buyers who then invite additional investments in amenities like shops and restaurants. Tanner Street near London Bridge station provides a perfect example of this regeneration. Whilst there are intellectual and financial rewards from being the first to invest in the area, having the agreement of other investors to invest too is more profitable as there is a shorter wait to see an uplift. Two or three firms that actively invest in the area creates a halo effect and prompts others to join the development. If a business is too small to do a major investment itself, it can still invest in older stock ideally within 400m of the new station. If that's not possible, gains can be enjoyed up to a mile from the station.

As this study shows, the land value uplift merry-go-round continues thanks to the generosity of the tax payer. The gains go to the landowners. Whilst this is something that must be changed if we want to create a fair entrepreneurial economy, the mechanism can be relied upon to generate positive investment returns if people buy land and property near major capital projects.

To maximise returns, investors should look for the following:

1. Does the project reduce travel times?
2. Does the project help people move from low opportunity areas to high opportunity areas? Or is it a road/rail to nowhere?
3. Is the area adjacent to already prosperous areas?
4. If it's a relatively deprived area, are there coherent funded plans to develop other public amenities such as schools, GPs surgeries, parks, etc. and to improve areas of deprivation?
5. Does the area have older housing stock that could be renovated or demolished to create higher density, modern housing?
6. Are a number of investors making purchases in the area? [First mover advantage is overrated in most investment situations].

Chapter 6

The Treasury Albatross

Major problems with financing public infrastructure stem from the nature of the tax system. The distortions have evolved over two centuries, which means that the public has grown to live with them. This means that the reforms we need are not likely to be introduced without an understanding of the historical twists and turns that brought us to the present crisis in public finance. A brief review of the background will be helpful.

Conservative governments in the 19th century set the scene for a cannibalistic system of taxation that attacked the capitalist system at its heart – the capacity to add value to the nation's wealth. Those governments championed the interests of an aristocratic culture that was parasitic on people who earned their living.

This was the century in which government tax philosophy evolved in a way that would impose artificial constraints on the factory-based system of producing wealth. People who were willing to work and invest were actively discouraged from delivering all the goods and services that their customers wanted. That tax philosophy also distorted the scale of people's savings. The result was a social and economic system that under-performed by enormous margins. Despite their ingenuity, people were discouraged from maximising their full potential as human beings. *Unemployment, poverty and nightmare housing were not the consequence of capitalism. They were the result of government policies that disempowered people.*

Nothing changed in the 20th century. Socialist governments tested their doctrines on hundreds of millions of people, but they did not alter the way in which public services were financed. But thanks to the perverse tax system, the *scale* of social and economic problems increased. Governments – both Conservative and Socialist – tried to moderate these problems, but they did so by imposing even higher burdens of taxation on people. This strategy, of trying to buy their way out of poverty and homelessness, was doomed from the outset. The policies, based on raising the burden of conventional taxes, merely strengthened the dead hand of government.

Economists have now calculated that the people of Britain are prevented from producing goods and services to the tune of more than £400 billion *every year*! Table 6:1 is based on a study by David Smith, the chief economist of a firm of London stockbrokers. He concluded that the UK economy could have produced more than 50% more than it delivered to consumers in 2000. That it did not do so Smith attributed to the tax system favoured by democratically-elected governments. This loss represents a hemorrhage which far exceeds what government requires to upgrade hospitals and schools and pay for all the nurses and teachers Britain needs. *This is an annual loss of around £7,000 for every man, woman and child in Britain.* It is no consolation to know that the losses are double or more in the G7 countries.

Table 6:1 Estimated effects on economic growth of increases in public spending since 1960			
	Change In Public Spending Burden 1960 1998 (%)	Estimated Impact on Annual Economic Growth (%)	How much higher output would have been in 2000 with 1980 spending levels (%)
Australia	11.7	-1.6	88
Canada	16.1	-2.2	138
France	19.7	-2.7	188
Germany	14.5	-2.0	118
Italy	19.0	-2.6	178
Ireland	9.6	-1.3	68
Japan	19.4	-2.6	183
New Zealand	20.2	-2.7	196
UK	8.0	-1.1	54
United States	5.8	-0.8	37
Source: David B. Smith, *Public Rags or Private Riches?* London: Politeia, 2001, p.17.			

Charade of the "Best Value" Policy

Mayor Livingstone prefers to pay for more trains and modernised stations by borrowing from the bond market, since this would ultimately cost taxpayers less money than under the proposals favoured by the Treasury.

The ultimate reality, however, is that most taxpayers will carry part of the costs even though they derive no value from the network of underground trains in the capital. This is neither fair nor efficient. It delivers a result that is not consistent with either capitalist efficiency or socialist fairness. The big-time losers are the residents of the capital, who find themselves locked into a stacked-deck gamble:

- Some property owners will be undeservedly rewarded with windfall fortunes.
- The living standards of the majority of dwellers in the capital, however, will be arbitrarily retarded.

How this happens became an inescapable part of my investigation.

The first task is to explain to the unworldly economists in the Treasury that it is possible to deliver a transport solution that combines fairness and efficiency. Without the policy which I shall describe, however, the economy will continue to fail to achieve its full growth potential. If changes are not introduced, *blame must be laid squarely at the door of the Treasury, which is the guardian of economic policy.*

Let's look at the evidence for the indictment that can be brought against the government and its economic advisers.

- New Labour has instructed local governments to be efficient in their financial dealings. They call it the Best Value Policy. Before preaching to others, however, central government should critically examine its own performance. Does the taxpayer get Best Value from the policies administered by the Treasury? Government is extremely inefficient. It raises revenue in a way that destroys the productive potential of the economy by a full 50%!

If the government fails to collect the revenue that is created by publicly funded services and investments, it has to use alternative methods for raising revenue. That is why it has had to invent techniques like Value Added Tax, which penalise people for going to work to earn their wages.

These taxes are unique in one particular way. Unlike the revenue from the rental income that flows from land, taxes on incomes from labour and capital distort the economy. In plain language, taxes kill the golden goose. That is just about as insane as you can get – *and we pay politicians to operate and protect that system!*

We saw that the under-production of goods and services estimated by David Smith was of the order of £428bn. (*see Table 6:1*). An alternative method for calculating the loss was used by two American professors of economics. Using data from 1993, they asked the question: how much more would the British economy have produced if government had raised its revenue from the rent of land rather than people's wages and the profits from their capital investments? The estimate is given in Table 6:2. The UK economy would have been larger by a little more than $700 bn. at the rate of exchange prevailing in 2000. That was a loss of about £440bn. These two estimates, by economists David Smith and Nicolaus Tideman, translate into a loss for every man, woman and child in Britain of about £7,500, or £30,000 for a family of parents and two children.[1]

Table 6:2 G7: Tax-Sponsored gain in Net Domestic Product by switching from old (O) to new (N) revenue policy: $ Billion			
	1993(O)	1993 (N)	Gain
USA	5494	7045	1552
Canada	490	769	279
France	937	1847	910
Germany	1178	2220	1042
Italy	892	1741	849
Japan	2134	3758	1624
UK	883	1594	711

Source: T. Nicolaus Tideman & Florenz Plassmann, in Harrison (Ed.), *The Losses of Nations*, pp.146–174.

The PPP formula is not a departure that will make a difference to this disgraceful situation. It is an unprincipled formula for the Treasury to avoid its responsibilities, the latest fashionable dodge to avoid having to reform public administration on the basis of time-honoured principles.

[1] Fred Harrison, "The Pathology of Taxation", *Geo* philos, Spring 2001, No. 01(1), pp. 145–150.

Governments will continue to preside over chaotic systems of public administration for so long as they refuse to redefine the legitimate boundaries between the public and private sectors.

The Treasury preserves its power by obscuring the boundaries between the activities that are of genuine social concern, only, and which therefore ought to be restricted to the public sphere (such as defence of the realm, and enforcement of the law); and those that are the business of the private sector (such as transporting people and freight around the country). The obsolete economic ideology, while inflicting a high price on taxpayers, is the protectionist tool for safeguarding the privileges of the patricians who exercise power in HM Treasury.

With the correct redefinition of the boundaries – which must include the reappraisal of property rights and public finance – it would be possible for surface transport to be delivered by private firms as efficiently as air travel by private airlines.

My proposal that property rights must be addressed is one that tends to be avoided by the British public, which has been cowed into thinking that all the fundamental issues of philosophy have been settled. But the private entrepreneurs bidding for access to the Underground know that they have to jealously guard their private property rights (*see Box 6:1*). I do not blame them for that. But it is also time for someone to champion the public interest. There ought not to be a conflict of interest between the two. In fact, as I shall explain, the two can work more effectively together if we introduce the idea of justice into the tax system.

Box 6:1
Ownership Rights down the Tube

Treasury civil servants invented and sold the concept of the Public-Private Partnership to the New Labour government Tracks, signalling and stations would be split into three parcels, to be run by private consortia for 30 years, while a public body would be responsible for running the trains.

The private consortia were supposed to bear the risk and invest about £7 billion to upgrade the underground network. They would then charge London Underground for running its trains. They would also receive a Treasury subsidy.

Critics argued that the performance targets were 5% below current service levels, so the private consortia were sure to pocket handsome bonuses but would have little incentive to raise the quality of the tube's service to passengers.

When Transport Commissioner Bob Kiley insisted that the network should be run under a unified management system, one of the prospective investors complained that this would "impinge on our rights of ownership".*

At no time during the negotiations was there discussion about the rights of ownership to the enhanced – and unearned – values that flow from publicly-financed investment in the capital's transport network.

* Joanna Walters & Nick Mathiason, "A deal gone down the Tube", *The Observer*, March 4, 2001.

2024 Update

Perhaps the best update to a chapter entitled 'The Treasury Albatross', would be to consider the comments of the Transport Minister, Steve Norris, who gained final approval for the Jubilee Line Extension. The JLE become one the most successful transport projects in living memory. He states the following:

Steve Norris:

There's one consistent element to the challenges we faced getting the JLE across the line and the approach now taken to all the other major projects: HM Treasury.

For generations, this country has been massively held back by their malign influence. It's right that they rigorously examine all spending applications. However, its default position, regardless of the value of the project, is expressed in Liam Byrne's now infamous letter to his successor as Chief Secretary to the Treasury – "I'm sorry, there's no money."

Even though Gordon Brown famously declared that he would spend on investment, his officials found a way of just saying no. I had taken the original Crossrail 1 Bill through an all-party Commons committee in 1995. They said they were convinced the project would be enormously valuable to London but were equally convinced that the Treasury would not fund it. Consequently, they turned the project down. The Labour opposition used this against the Tory government during the next election promising to revive the project in their 1997 manifesto. But it was only in 2009 that work actually began. This was a colossal waste in potential productivity and delayed the regeneration of blighted areas of the South.

With the Jubilee Line Extension, the Treasury put as many obstacles in the way as they could. "Surrey Canal, minister?" (It's not in Surrey and there's no canal) ... "The Greenwich Peninsula is a contaminated coaling site ... What's the point of going to places nobody lives in?" And so on. They were delighted when Olympia & York, the Reichmann brother's investment vehicle which owned Canary Wharf, went into administration. "Well," the Treasury told us, "You'll just have to get the £400m which Olympia & York had committed to contribute to the build cost. If you can't get it from them, you'll just have to get that from the creditor banks."

What they had not realised, but the 14 creditor banks all knew, was that, in administration, the Canary Wharf asset was worthless, but with the JLE it would be worth a billion dollars. All 14 duly and willingly signed up. That still wasn't enough.

Eventually, I had to threaten the then Chief Secretary Michael Portillo that if he didn't approve the project, I, having curated a large selection of quotes from John Major that we had slipped into his speeches all praising the JLE, would resign and tell the world that the Prime Minister was a downright liar. That had the desired effect.

We are now in the crazy position where the Treasury has insisted on delaying spending on the Lower Thames Crossing and HS2 where the only known impact is that the cost in both cases will rise. The Bakerloo Line extension should have started years ago. That would have opened up a hugely deprived area very close to central London. It is great value for money and the route is clearly identified. Yet it has no start date.

Northern Powerhouse Rail would do more to regenerate the Northern cities than any other project and is yet to start despite being a known worthwhile project since 2009.

The UK Treasury knows the price of everything and the value of nothing. Liz Truss may be wrong on a great many things, but she was absolutely right that reforming the Treasury is the biggest single change any government could make that would revitalise the whole United Kingdom. Harold Wilson tried and failed with the Department of Economic Affairs in the 1960s, and the real question is whether Rishi Sunak will have the time and energy to do it. Sadly, for all I rate the man, I doubt it.

Chapter 7

The Win-Win Public Finance

Why do I, as a landowner, advocate a tax policy that would target my income from land? There are two reasons. First, everyone would get richer if we got rid of deadweight taxes. Secondly, the negative influence of taxation on the property industry out of which I make my living is crippling. Builders bear a heavy risk, part of which they shift on to their workers. That is why we rely so much on subcontractors, which is not a secure arrangement for people who support families. Taxation is directly responsible for fragmenting the construction sector; which then imposes stresses on people's lives that lead to the fragmentation of society at large.

Ultimately, society's failure to value its land and use is also responsible for homelessness and poor quality housing. But there are no sustainable solutions for dealing with the perpetual social crisis within the plans administered by governments and their bureaucracies. *The fundamental solution is to harness the power of the free market, by adopting tax reforms in which everyone wins.*

Ultimately, however, responsibility for the crushing ceiling that is lowered onto the economy must be laid at the door of Parliament. If politicians seek the mandate to act as the guardians of other people's lives, in Parliament, they ought to provide themselves with all the information they need to discharge their duties. If MPs were to consult Hansard, the record of all speeches in the House of Commons, they would find ample evidence that Parliament had been warned time and again that it was propping up an indefensible system for raising revenue from the public (*see Box 7:1*). That information is certainly not being provided to the electorate, who need it if they are to make informed judgments on what is in their best private and social interests.

Box 7:1
Bridge to a fortune

Labour MP Andrew MacLaren devoted his Parliamentary career to urging the House of Commons to reform the way it agreed to fund public projects. He insisted that the electorate had the right to treat community-created rents as the source of public revenue. Otherwise, that public value ended up in the pockets of landowners. One of his examples related to a road bridge that was to be sited near Charring Cross underground station. He calculated who would be the major winners:

> "There was a sum of £14.5 million to give work to the unemployed, and probably, if this Bill had been passed, that scheme would have been pushed through without public examination and without any full examination by this House. Out of that £14.5 million, £11.5 million was to be handed over to the landowners, to remove them out of the way" (*Hansard*, July 11 1930, Col. 830).

According to a biography of MacLaren,* the MP never tired of explaining to his fellow MPs that the projected increase in land values as a result of investments such as the one in the proposed bridge approached the same figure as such schemes estimated costs.

* John Young, *Justice: An Enduring Quest*, London: Shepheard-Walwyn, forthcoming.

But politicians do come and go: their officials – like those in the Treasury – have a longer shelf-life, and they ought to know better. They ought to offer in-coming governments the advice that serves the interests of the whole nation, not just the private interests of an obsolete aristocracy which had biased taxation in favour of their private interests. They are, after all, not political appointees. They are the servants of the nation. That is why the dead hand of the Treasury is particularly woeful.

When New Labour was elected in 1997, Gordon Brown promised that the Treasury would adopt fiscally "prudent" policies, and that it would be transparent in its dealings with taxpayers.

This word *prudent* was borrowed from New Zealand, along with policies that New Labour introduced. The most notable was the decision to make the Bank of England independent. This connection with New

Zealand is important, because it offers us valuable historical insights into what is likely to happen after New Labour has exhausted itself.

Gordon Brown claimed that, by making the Bank of England independent, the temptation to use monetary policy for political purposes would be removed. So the British reform was modelled on New Zealand's Fiscal Responsibility Act (1994). This law specifies five principles of responsible fiscal management. Three out of the five principles invoke the word *prudent*.

- Achieve a prudent level of public debt
- Maintain public debt at a prudent level
- Manage prudently the risks facing the Crown

That word became the mantra for Gordon Brown's speeches. His budget pronouncements in the House of Commons is peppered with the word.

Another word imported from the New Zealand political agenda of the previous two decades was *transparency*. The New Zealand government decided to open up its democracy, by making its decisions accessible to the electorate. Gordon Brown loves that word: he went on to preach *prudence* and *transparency* to the Asian "tigers" when they got into trouble! But what has his record been like back home? The *Financial Times* took him to task in its editorial on March 2, 2001. It accused the Chancellor of the Exchequer of reducing "Budget transparency to a new low". The evidence is transparent enough!

- Important tax changes are silently glossed over by Mr. Brown. In his 2000 budget speech, for example, he omitted reference to the changes to double tax relief for multinational companies, "which risked making the UK an unattractive place for corporate location".
- Statistics continue to be manipulated. "The Budget documentation has been filled with political point-scoring rather than factual analysis."
- Most damagingly, from the point of view of democratic debate, "there has been a continued tendency to classify the collection of revenue as anything other than taxation". Mr. Brown "boasts of lower corporate tax rates and forgets that the abolition of the dividend tax credit has raised the level of taxation on corporate income".

If people are baffled by the phraseology that even taxes highly-trained accountants and lawyers, what chance do ordinary taxpayers have when it comes to forming a judgment on a government's record? The *Financial Times* was correct to conclude: "Mr. Brown must remember that this obfuscation harms a sensible taxation debate and encourages tax wheezes, which will ultimately harm the economy".

The damage which Mr. Brown inflicted on the economy began the day he walked into the Treasury and decided to spin for himself the image of a "tough" chancellor. His cherry-picking tour of the latest economic fashions around the world, and especially from the recent history of New Zealand, launched Britain on a phony path of reform that will one day end in tears. We can make this prediction on the basis of the outcome of events "down under".

Lamb to the slaughter is the way I would describe what happened to Gordon Brown, when he fell for the doctrines that were developed in New Zealand.

So far as they went, the economic ideas that originated in the 1980s were sensible: they certainly conveyed the impression that politicians had finally learnt their lesson. But they were partial solutions, which meant that for many people, the medicine turned out to be worse than the disease.

Tax reform was on the agenda. There was no doubt that New Zealand needed radical changes in the way revenue was raised for the public sector, but was the *right kind* of reform introduced?

We saw from Table 6:1 (*page 50*) that the burden of taxation over the 20 years of "reforms" helped to reduce the rate of growth of the New Zealand economy by an average of 2.7% a year below what it would have been. The economy would be nearly 200% larger if the tax-take had remained at its 1960 level.

- The Organisation for Economic Cooperation and Development (OECD) now places New Zealand near the bottom of the league table for *per capita* incomes – 25th out of the 29 economies that it monitors. The average *per capita* income was NZ$26,125 in 2000,[1] when New Zealand was overtaken by the relatively backward economy of Spain for the first time.

[1] OECD, *New Zealand*, Paris, 1999.

Like enterprising people everywhere, many New Zealanders (8% of the population) moved to or remained in Australia!

The economists who presided over the reforms were at first jubilant about what they perceived to be the improvements to the New Zealand economy. One of them was Donald Brash, a lapsed Marxist and contemporary of mine at university in New Zealand. Twenty years ago, he was rejected twice by the electorate and failed to enter Parliament. However, when Parliament wished to delegate power and responsibility (= blame!) for the economy, it gave Brash the interest rate joystick in 1988 as Governor of the Reserve Bank of New Zealand! He flew to London in 1996 to crow about the results of the New Zealand experiment, but he could not help identifying some paradoxical outcomes. One related to taxation.

- Although tax rates were reduced, and the structure of taxation was simplified – all in the name of taking less from the people who create the wealth – "total government spending was over 41% of GDP at the beginning of [the 1990s], somewhat higher than the ratio in the mid-1980s".[2]

The reforms had begun in 1984 – and within 10 years, the tax-take *increased*! The reason, of course, is that most of the benefits of the tax changes went to the well-heeled, without introducing the structural reforms that would enable the unemployed and those on low wages to improve their situation.

Who is to blame for the decline in people's living standards?

Responsibility has to be laid at the door of the successive governments that chose to stick with a tax regime that undermines people's capacity to produce all the wealth they want.

Politicians get away with what they are doing because of their ability to wrap mystical meanings into ordinary words. Take the phrase "broadening the tax base". Government treasuries love that phrase, and the public has been schooled to think that it implies a perfectly reasonable policy goal. But when we translate that phrase into honest words, a quite different meaning emerges. Broad-based taxes are *stealth* taxes. They are designed to pluck the golden goose without the victim

[2] Donald T. Brash, *New Zealand's Remarkable Reforms*, London: IEA, 1996, p.38.

knowing what is going on. Doesn't taxation by stealth offend against the principle of transparency?

This is how Donald Brash described the effect of the decision to create "a broad-based value-added tax", known as the Goods and Services Tax (it started with a single rate of 10%, which was soon raised to 12.5%):

> The unusual thing about that tax is that the Government was willing to include everything except financial services in the tax net – food, medical services, books, children's clothing, the lot – all at the same rate, recognising that only by so doing would economic distortions be avoided and the compliance costs entailed in collecting the tax be minimised.[3]

So people on the lowest incomes had to pay the tax, while financiers were exempted! Is it surprising that the poor became even more dependent on state hand-outs? Is it surprising that the under-class created by tax policy had to be supported by an ever-increasing level of tax-take?

But is it true that economic distortions were avoided? I don't think so. Today, according to my calculation, for every man, woman and child in New Zealand – which has a population of 3.6m – the annual loss of income is of the order of NZ$52,000 (or about £18,500) for one reason alone: the way in which the government *chooses* to raise the revenue it needs to spend on public services.

It is important to stress that these losses are *under*-estimates. This is because they are calculated on the basis of retaining the structure of the tax system as it existed in 1960. Even that level of taxation was damaging the economy, because of the nature of the taxes that the government employed.

- At the end of 20 years of systematic reforms, New Zealand families with the lowest incomes in this small-population/land-rich country, were priced out of owning their homes. Despite low interest rates, and the requirement to pay small deposits for a

[3] *Ibid.*, p.28.

mortgage, they found that they were excluded from the housing market. There is one reason only for this: the price of land.

Who is to blame for this social exclusion from the basic right to earn a home of one's own? Aren't people working hard enough?

In the Auckland region, raising the deposit for a house used to require 1.6 times the annual household income of a low-income family. By 1998, this had increased to more than 2.1 times the annual household income. So as the "reforms" bit into the economy – changing laws, institutions, people's expectations, provision of public services to vulnerable groups in the community (*see Box 7:2*) – so more and more people fell behind in their ability to put roofs over their heads. Yet 20 years earlier, in 1978, Labour had promised that if elected no one would be required to pay more than a fifth of their income in repayment of both mortgage capital and interest.

Box 7:2
New Zealand "reform" strategy

Reforms launched in 1984 turned New Zealand into one of the most open and market-oriented countries among the richest nations. According to conventional political wisdom, privatisation and deregulation would jump-start a higher rate of growth driven by improved productivity. Public enterprises were sold off, and government coffers were enriched to the tune of NZ$16.6 billion.

Politicians really believed in the integrity of their strategies. This self-satisfaction found its expression in the Fiscal Responsibility Act 1994. The law was supposed to improve the government's performance in taxation (words like *fairness* and *transparency* were used to convey the impression of morality and managerial efficiency).* The reforms were supposed to raise growth to 3.5% to 5%. But the guiding principles made no provision for either

- revealing how much money people were losing because of the negative impact of tax policies; or
- exposing the unfair – irresponsible – way in which government discriminately enriched some people through public investments that raised land values.*

---

* OECD, *New Zealand*, Paris: OECD, 1999, p.124.

There is one explanation only why the price of houses outstrips the increase in people's incomes: land in the right locations is scarce. Owners can push prices up, and under the present tax regime, people's disposable incomes are reduced to levels that price them out of the housing market. Successive New Zealand governments – both local and national – have chosen not to stick with the one policy that would avoid this outcome. They have chosen to shift their fiscal base away from the unearned rent of land and onto people's wages and savings (*see Box 7:3*).

If taxation did not inhibit people from producing the incomes they want – and which are possible, given current technological and entrepreneurial realities – there would have been no involuntary poverty in New Zealand, or inability to buy family homes. Under the rational system of public finance, the wages of those on the bottom rungs would have been much higher, in real terms. This is because there would be a shortage of labour, relative to capital, so wages would benefit relatively more from the new prosperity. And the problems peculiar to the land market (which is a monopolistic market) would be neutralised by the tax system. This means that people would be rewarded for their inputs into the system of wealth production. No-one would be enriched on the back of their idleness and other people's effort.

Box 7:3
New Zealand's land-tax record

The British colony adopted the sound principles of public finance over 120 years ago. Governor Sir George Grey discussed the theory of land taxation with philosopher John Stuart Mill, whose phrase – that landowners get rich even as they sleep – is a famous citation in the academic literature.

In 1878, as Prime Minister, Grey introduced a land tax both to finance the huge investments that were required in public infrastructure, but also to break up the large estates that hindered the settlement of migrants on family farms.

In 1922, the land tax yielded about 10% of the Budget. By 1989, that tax yielded only 0.4% of the Budget "and was commonly regarded as an antiquated irritant".*

The fall out of favour of land values at the national level was not echoed locally, where (in 1982) land-value rates constituted 80% of local government revenue. But despite the democratic popularity of land-rent based taxation, local politicians ran rearguard actions to switch to a property tax that was also imposed on the value of buildings. So by the end of the century, the land-value proportion had dropped to about 40%.

*   Robert D. Keall, "New Zealand", in R.V. Andelson (ed.), *Land-Value Taxation Around the World*, 3rd edn., Oxford: Blackwells, 2000, p.423.

But under the conventional tax regimes, the gap between the rich and the poor will continue to widen. The stake is being driven ever deeper into the heart of society, as landowners reap an increasing share of the wealth generated by working people. Orthodox economists show no interest in this tax-wedge driven process of social exclusion, but Figure 7:1 shows what will happen over the next 20 years in Australia on the basis of current trends. Notice that the share going to wages has been constant for most of the last 50 years. And in an open economy, migrating capital means that competition ensures that the owners of capital do not take a growing share of the nation's wealth. Result: it is the landowner who pockets the difference.

This brief review of New Zealand's recent history gives us a taste of the outcome we can expect under Gordon Brown's stewardship at HM Treasury.

New Zealand could have been a beacon of hope to the rest of the world. It has a substantial historical record of support for treating rent as public revenue. But while voters generally accepted the wisdom of placing the tax on land – and removing it from their investments in improvements on the land – the politicians flouted the popular preference and gradually eroded the democratic will.

The failed New Zealand experiment could now retard the need for more de-regulation and liberalisation of the economy. The failed reforms have prejudiced people against the market. As one commentator noted, New Zealand

> Thatcherised before Thatcher, Reaganised faster than Reagan. Rightwing economists the world over flocked to the south Pacific to hail the Kiwis' wisdom in privatising faster and more furiously than any country in the world. In a few, breakneck years in the mid-80s they did it all: deregulation, tax cuts, selling off the state-owned family silver.[4]

Predictably, the reaction has set in. Now the demand is to renationalise. One of the targets in the sights of the Labour/Alliance coalition government in 2001 was Tranz Rail.

> They are now eyeing the railway network which, like Britain's, was sold off in the last decade. The privatised service, Tranz Rail, has been deluged with the same criticisms heard in Britain – over everything from declining safety standards to abandoned rural services. The papers call it Tranz Fail.[5]

It is too early to predict the outcome, but in the case of the Wisconsin-owned Tranz Rail, it seems that the government has a trump card up its sleeve. The government is

---

[4] Jonathan Freedland, "Ready to renationalise", *The Guardian* (London), February 14, 2001.
[5] *Ibid.*

Figure 7:1 Projections to 2020 of selected Australian economic trends.

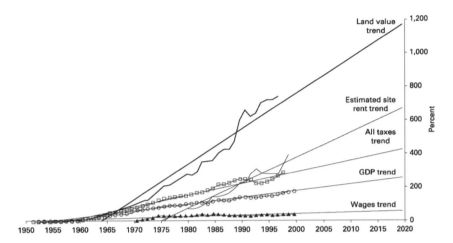

Source: Tony O'Brien, "The Pathology of Income Maldistribution: an Index of the Wealth-Poverty Gap in Australia (1951–200)" Geophilos, Autumn 2000, No. 00(1), p.65.

reminding Tranz Rail … that the government still owns the land under the track and that it is quite willing to run services the firm deems unprofitable. Translation: Labour is ready to shove the fat cats to one side and renationalise a chunk of the railway.

Renationalisation is not the modern answer. There is a principled solution that divides property rights on the basis of justice, and a public finance system that is faithful to people's sense of fairness. In essence, the correct solution is to apply pressure on people who use land (whether they are owners or not: *use* is what matters), within the framework of the free market.

Ordinary people would understand this, but if their creative energies are to be unharnessed, they will have to challenge the politicians. They will have to inform themselves on the facts, and examine all the policy options, so that they can then exercise their democratic rights.

Some people might think my proposal is impossible – because it means tampering with the law. And once lawyers become involved, all kinds of chicanery are possible. In fact, the task of changing the law is easier than you might think.

A ready packaged solution exists. Herbert Morrison, the grandfather of Peter Mandelson – one of the architects of New Labour's 1997 electoral success – sponsored the London Rating (Site Values) Bill in 1938 which would have placed London's revenue-raising system on a rational basis (*see plate 4*). The government managed to disallow this popular proposal on technical grounds. The Bill does not require much work to modify it so that it could be reintroduced by the government, working with Mayor Ken Livingstone.

Whether government can find the courage to adopt this reform depends largely on enough people being willing to mobilise their democratic power to insist on change. A close scrutiny of conventional political ideology is necessary, if we are to evaluate correctly the policies that could transform the public sector into a creative partner working with the private sector.

In my view, a change in the style and content of government is not an optional extra. The challenges of the 21st century could leave Britain behind, just as New Zealand is now slipping back in the income stakes.

In calling for a sweeping change to taxation, I am aware that many interests have to be taken into account. There again, I am also aware that many of these interests are ignored under the current regime. Take, for example, the way in which investment in a railway track or road increases the value of land. We need to acknowledge that these investments also shift the geographical dispersion of economic activity, to some people's disadvantage. As mobile enterprises concentrate near stations, the economic base elsewhere is weakened. As firms move to the more productive locations, they abandon other communities. So, a reduction in the production costs in the newly thriving areas is matched by an increase in the production costs elsewhere. The clustering of economic activity around motorway junctions or railway stations is often at the expense of what were once thriving communities. Government must compensate for this effect, but not by handing out other people's money. The rent-as-public-revenue policy balances everyone's interests through the market, and without the need for subsidies or government programmes to support weakened localities.

2024 Update

Don's prediction that Gordon Brown "*launched Britain on a phony path of reform that will one day end in tears*," turned out to be accurate. The borrowing levels of the UK during Brown's tenure were broadly in line with other nations enjoying an enormous land cycle boom (higher tax receipts matched with higher spending so the GDP to borrowing percentage stayed roughly the same). Borrowing then rose massively after the crash as the taxpayer was forced to bail out the banks when the cycle collapsed. This is exactly as Fred Harrison predicted in the books *Boom Bust (2005)* and *The Chaos Makers (1997)*.

Brown's greatest distinctions as Chancellor was the sell-off of the UK's gold reserves at the absolute lowest end of the market, costing British citizens billions, and his repeated claims to have eliminated boom-bust. The last time he said this in public was during his final budget before the biggest financial bust in 80 years. He said repeatedly that his economic policy was "prudence for a purpose" and that purpose was to "get rid of boom and bust from the economy". His measure of his success was essentially the rate of inflation, and he relied on raising interest rates to lower it. This made no difference to a housing market where gains were 20% a year but were catastrophic for many small and medium sized enterprises, especially exporters who relied on borrowing to finance their businesses.

Brown had all the information he needed to actually stop the Boom Bust cycle. Not only had he commissioned studies from his own staff into the nature of business cycles, Fred Harrison had spent more than 10 years trying to warn the Labour government of the crash that was guaranteed to happen if they didn't change the structure of the economy. Fred even had a personal briefing with Shriti Vadera, Gordon Brown's economic adviser in the Treasury. The only effect it had was for him to receive a hand-written message from Alastair Campbell, Tony Blair's fixer, to "Cheer up!" (and "stop going on about the future crash").

In Brown's 2003 budget speech, he shared his own team's research showing that the volatile housing market had been most responsible for our lower economic performance compared with our European neighbours. This shows he could have ignored Fred's research and entreaties and still had what he needed to actually be the transformational chancellor he claimed to be.

In his March 21, 2007 budget speech, only 6 months before Northern Rock's collapse in September 2007 (and the beginning of the financial crash), he claimed, "... *we will not return to the old boom and bust*".

His self-congratulatory speech in which he praises his "historic achievements," months before the UK property market crash that lunged the country into a depression, is a clear indication of his delusion.

https://publications.parliament.uk/pa/cm200607/cmhansrd/cm070321/debtext/70321-0004.htm

Brown was so enraptured by his deluded self-perception as the most successful chancellor in 200 years (according to his 2007 Budget speech) that he took credit for the prosperity that came from the property boom and managed to get himself crowned "hero of the hour" by Paul Krugman for "rescuing" the world from the financial collapse when the crash inevitably happened.

https://www.reuters.com/article/uk-financial-brown-analysis-idUKTRE49D5Z520081014

This deluded self-perception continued after he became Prime Minister. During PM's Questions in December 2008, Brown uttered the words, "*We not only saved the world ...*" to much delight and derision from the opposition. He claimed it was a mistake and that he meant to say, "We had not only saved the banks and led the world ...". Gordon Brown saved nothing. Brown and his Treasury team had all the information and the opportunity needed to eliminate the boom bust cycle. He completely wasted the best opportunity since the People's Budget in 1909 to genuinely transform our economy.

---

* More on this can be found in Fred Harrison's book, *'Boom Bust': House Prices, Banking and the Depression of 2010.*

Chapter 8

The London Blueprint

Local governments, because of their powers over land-use, have a major responsibility in the new deal that I envisage. They ought to be more responsive to what people want, while taking into account the responsibility for discharging social and environmental obligations. I am confident that, under the new approach to public finance, communities would automatically "shake down" to their full private and social potential with the minimum of political interference.

For example, the revenue system based on land values, if it is sensitively linked to market rents, automatically reduces the rental charges payable by people in areas that lose businesses. As rents drop, so these areas acquire a new attraction – it is cheaper to establish infant enterprises here. This leads to the renewal of a locality even as firms are attracted out by public investment elsewhere. This is the evolutionary approach to change that allows enterprising people to retain both their private incomes and their dignities.

We also have to admit that new systems of transportation may not generate benefits. If they fail to provide the quality of service that people need – a system appropriately integrated into the communities they are supposed to serve – the investment will not necessarily raise land values. The land market is a sensitive barometer of the efficiency with which government and the Treasury designs its projects. Land values, when treated as the source of public revenue, becomes a discipline to guide investment decisions. If a project is not going to raise land values sufficiently to pay for capital costs, a question mark has to be placed against it.

That is why the private sector component to these considerations is vital. Private investors are not as ready to throw their money away, as bureaucrats are ready to throw away taxpayers' money.

London could lead the world with this reform under the leadership of its new Mayor. Ken Livingstone has announced that he wants the capital to grow by nearly 10% to 8.1 million people in the 15 years to 2016. The city's strategic plan, announced on May 8 2001, will be challenged by the way in which it addresses the problem of land and rent.

The Mayor wants an alliance with property companies. He offers them the opportunity to build high-density residential developments, in return for a guarantee that at least 50% of the new homes will be rented at affordable prices.

The plan projects the need for over 33,000 new homes every year over 15 years. The biggest developments will be on brownfield sites in the East End, around the interchange with the channel tunnel rail link at Stratford, and in corridors leading to Stansted, Gatwick and Heathrow airports.

Under the Mayor's plan, developers would be encouraged to provide offices and homes near big new transport intersections created by the construction of cross-London rail lines.

This combination of locations and development aspirations is an explosive cocktail that will certainly drive up the rental income of owners who currently possess the key sites. Should they pocket that unearned income, or should the Mayor now go to Parliament and make the case for the recycling of land values to pay for the public services?

Mr. Livingstone knows there is a connection between lifestyle and land values. He says:

> People like living in urban areas, close to the facilities and services they need. That is one of the reasons why house prices in Knightsbridge and Islington – some of the densest urban areas in London – are so high. We must ensure that London exemplifies urban renaissance by developing at higher densities in more attractive urban environments, linked to public transport services.[1]

The Mayor's plan calls for London to retain a larger share of tax revenues in order to increase investment in the capital's infrastructure. That call is not precise enough. I have stressed that the key is not how much revenue is raised, but how it is raised. Mayor Livingstone needs to factor this blueprint into his plans for London.

---

[1] John Carvel, "Mayor's blueprint for London", *The Guardian*, May 8, 2001.

London's economy is central to the UK economy. Britain's citizens paid Chancellor Brown £50 bn more income tax than in 1997, yet London suffered the same or worse public services than the rest of the UK. Ferdinand Mount wrote in the *Sunday Times*:

> Despite the proportion of national income taken by the state under Labour edging up from 35% to 40%, anyone with eyes in their head can see that virtually all the public services in the UK are grotesquely under-financed, not only schools and hospitals, but universities, the armed services, the police and prison services, museums, the arts.[2]

Mount overlooks transport. Does he count it as a private service, despite the £180 bn state plan?

I challenge Mayor Livingstone, who resigned as an MP to concentrate on his mayoral duties, to put London's financing of services back on track.

The rest of the UK, and countries like New Zealand which deregulated at the end of the 20th century, would then have a model of how to elevate themselves to new heights of prosperity driven by the blueprint offered by London.

Everyone agrees that London needs a viable underground rail system. The way to finance the infrastructure, which will run into billions of pounds, is for the Greater London Authority to be given the responsibility for financing the loans by recycling the land value that will be generated by an improved service.

Bonds and taxation can be linked through the land-rents of London. To achieve this, London could borrow an idea from the US, where Special Benefit Districts are created to pay for specific public projects such as the construction of a road. These investments enhance the value of land in the catchment areas; they raise the quality of the lives of residents – so why shouldn't they pay for the benefits they receive? London could establish a special levy on the rental value of each site in the capital to finance the bonds that would provide the cash flow that is required to upgrade the Tube.

As a landowner near a proposed brand new or enhanced Tube station, I can see the advantage of my firm owning Tube bonds, received

---

[2] Ferdinand Mount, "What have they done", *Sunday Times Election Guide 2001*, May 13, 2001.

annually in exchange for my land levy. My land value would begin to climb, the moment the infrastructure improvement was announced. I might have the option to convert the bonds to equity or receive other rights, the scope for these and "ownership" being limited only by the creativity of our representatives on the project board of directors.

The Treasury would have to rethink its attitudes, because it would have to support changes in the law. But when all is said and done – Parliament represents the people, and the Treasury is at Her Majesty's (which means our) service.

The model of financing could be road-tested in London, and then applied generally as the heart of a strategic reform of the nation's public finances. It is a template which must be generalised to pay for public projects that deliver their benefits across the nation. The challenge is an immediate one. Take, for example, the announcement in January 2001 by the Strategic Rail Authority that it favoured a purpose-built railway for trains running at 200 to 225 mph. This would be the fastest in Europe, slashing journey times between major cities by a huge factor. Travelling north from London, journeys to Manchester or Leeds would come down to less than one hour 30 minutes, Newcastle to around two hours and Scotland to less than three hours. This would reduce everyone's costs. And that would increase house and commercial property prices across the country.

Under the current tax regime, reduced costs – which ought to be a blessing – is a two-edged sword that smites the weak and enriches the rich.

- The geographically disadvantaged North-East of England, for example, is heavily dependent on a good rail service to London. The North-east Chamber of Commerce chief executive, Michael Bird, emphasises that the business community "on the periphery of England ... [must] have superb links to the centre. We don't".[3]

But a 200 mph railway in the national interest could not be financed in isolation. The whole nation could not be turned into a Special Benefit District to raise the revenue to pay for this one project. The finance

[3] Chris Tighe, "Vital link for 'region on the periphery'", *Financial Times*, March 1, 2001.

would have to come out of a generalised system of land-rent revenue, collected by central government from the nation, and deployed in the national interest.

That is why an integrated tax system needs to be sensitively tuned to the taxable capacity of every region, every city, every locality, right down to every site in every street. An *ad valorem* charge on the stream of rental income that can be imputed to each site is the progressive revenue-raiser of the 21st century.

Wealthy firms and people occupy the most expensive locations. Incomes are linked to property values, which are directly associated with the volume and quality of the services that people want to "buy". The logic of this argument is illustrated, at the most abstract level, in Figure 8:1. This shows the average house price along a straight line drawn from London to the North. London has the greatest taxable capacity – as measured by the amount of money that people can *and do* pay for the privilege of occupying the sites that give them access to the services they want. Revenue obligations ought to fall away, in line with the decline in productivity, reaching their lowest levels in the peripheral locations where the price of land signals that taxable capacity is at its lowest.

Figure 8:1 Average House Prices, England (2000 Q4; £000s)

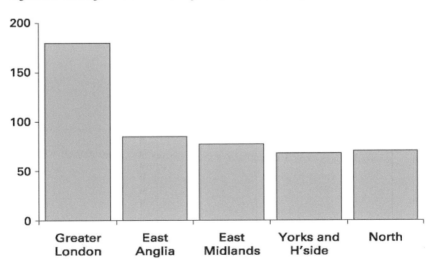

Source: HM Land Registry, *Residential Property Price Report*, London, 2000.

By establishing the practice of public finance that is grounded in the principles of both justice and efficiency, it becomes possible to create a public-private partnership that works – instead of one that corrupts (*see Box 8:1*). *There is no reason, now, why private enterprise should not run services like railways: there is no national security reason why government should be in charge of making the trains run on time, or keeping the carriages clean.* The leasehold agreements that could be struck would clearly differentiate private activity from public obligations. Everyone would know where the cut-off points were, in terms of obligations and money.

Box 8:1
The Road to Corruption

Essex property investor Tony Parker was shocked when he was exposed to the shady side of the economics of land-and-transportation.

He joined a group of financiers interested in a hotel development in Normandy, the selling point of which – promoted by Mayors and councillors from the region – was the close proximity of a new road being built to carry motorists from Northern France to the sunny South. On returning to England, he wrote:

"The chosen route for the road was not the optimum geographical route, but a wavy line that passed by several plots or land owned by the Mayors and their cronies. Present at our meetings was a French Ministry of Agriculture representative, there to give planning permission that might have otherwise been difficult to obtain . . .

"One of the Mayors owned a furniture shop on the proposed route which we valued at about £50,000. With the road in place and planning permission to turn the building into a three-star motel, the site was worth approximately £350,000. A more strategic route for the new road using the existing infrastructure would have missed this site by approximately 10 miles."

* Tony G. Parker, "Long and winding road to corruption", *Evening Standard*, March 19, 1999.

The whole system would be based on the equity we find in the markets, and the equity we find in the philosophy of justice.

- There would be no need for cap-in-hand search for subsidies from taxpayers; no sneaky smears against entrepreneurs, from politicians.
- The public could request special Tube trains, or New Year's Eve services, and be informed in advance of the likely cost of such public services, so that the benefits they received could be weighed against the costs.

Link this policy to a general reduction in the taxes that damage the health and wealth of the nation, whose compliance costs are so burdensome, and it would unite the kingdom even as democratic power was further devolved to the people.

People's freedoms are associated with the right to the property that they create by labour. The community's obligations to its members can be fulfilled only if it recovers that part of the total value of the nation that each of us produces in partnership with everyone else. The classical economists offered a forensically clear definition of that value. It is the income stream associated with land in all its forms – whether urban sites, fertile farmland, radio spectrum, sea lanes, the wind that drives mills, the base and precious ores in the bowels of the earth (*see Box 8:2*).

That income is designated as *economic rent*. This is a technical concept: it is not synonymous with the *commercial rents* that I charge my tenants, because they pay for the right to use my buildings, as well as the land. Professionals in the property market know how to distinguish between those two values.

If government can come to philosophical terms with the correct structure of property rights, it would have in the palm of its hands the solution to most of society's ills.

Solving the problem of paying for transport identifies the solution to an even greater problem – the instability of the economy. *My realisation that the greater than 100% gain for landowners with sites alongside new transport links led me to examine the mechanism of all land gains by landowners, and to reflect on the counterbalancing losses to the community.*

Once I had realised that there was a general connection between land, taxation and the business cycle, I understood that the correct financing of transport systems would also deliver the most powerful tool for countering the malignant effects of the boom/bust cycles.

Box 8:2
Archer's Time & Tide

Landowners don't rely exclusively on transport across dry land for their unearned riches. A bizarre example of how modes of transport enriches them was offered by Geoffrey Archer, the bestselling novelist and disgraced Tory politician. He has been rewarded by the sea lanes that originate from the ports of New Zealand.

In 1986 he paid £400,000 for 61 acres of waterfront land in Auckland.

As with all good land speculators, he was willing to bide his time.

That time came in 1995, when he was reportedly offered £3.1 million for the land that could be developed as residential properties. What had made the difference? New Zealand was set to win the America's Cup. If it did so, as victors New Zealand would host the next competition – and that would bump up the value of his land.

He was given hours to decide whether to pocket the bonanza – the prospective buyer wanted to clinch the deal before the sails were unfurled for the final race, because, otherwise, if the Kiwis won, the land might be worth even more!

Lord Archer decided to decline the offer. He had all the time in the world . . .

It was also clear that governments are unprincipled in their approach to disposing of taxpayers' money. This is highlighted by the incomplete approach employed by the Department of the Environment, Transport and the Regions. According to the National Audit Office:

> There is no clear and agreed methodology for calculating the monetary impacts of the wider benefits of public transport projects, such as the regeneration of local economies, so they are not usually included in monetary terms in the value for money assessments of such projects.[4]

The landowners who cash-in on the blind spot in the methodology are delighted, of course, because this leads government to generously

---

[4] National Audit Office, *The Channel Tunnel Rail Link*, London: Stationery Office, March 2001, p.33.

hand out taxpayers' money to make up the alleged financial deficits in public investment projects.

2024 Update

The 2000 house price data Don shared seems remarkable for what now appears to be such low prices. The following are the 2023 averages as shared by the UK Land Registry.

London	£527,979
East of England	£351,213
East Midlands	£248,678
Yorkshire and Humberside	£208, 867
North of England	£188, 332

https://www.gov.uk/government/statistics/uk-house-price-index-for-june-2023/uk-house-price-index-summary-june-2023

Whilst the prices have changed, and a portion of Ken Livingstone's plans for building along the Thames into Kent were successful, little else has changed (Crossrail excepted) and Don's arguments are equally valid.

The projects to connect the North are gridlocked and on current timing may never actually be completed. Politicians or the Treasury seem to find more excuses to delay the completion. They cite value and cost concerns but the real problem, as we hope you now see, is that we have public investment and private profit.

Don was right again even though it would have been much better for everyone if he had been proven wrong. Without change, more and more people are priced out of their own hometowns and are unable to access the gains that their taxes deliver, as they don't own property and land. The landowners are careful to ensure that no one ever speaks about the subsidies they receive through land value capture.

Chapter 9

Digging out more than the Jubilee Line

Every year, in late November or early December, I hold my Landlord's Lunch for directors and owners of businesses who are my tenants. So far, there have been 17 such lunches. One of them had the theme "Celebrate the Jubilee Line". Another was called "Why does everyone hate the Landlord?" My wife prepares the food and my family and friends serve the guests who, after listening to a brief speech, attack or defend landlords.

Tenants who have been with me for a while and know me as a resident landlord who keeps the buildings in good working order would agree that they get a fair exchange for their rent. They do their business, and I provide space with no directors' guarantees or deposits. I am happy to see them expand or shrink within my buildings according to how their business is doing.

Most of them also accept that, in addition to the rent I get from them, as taxpayers they have additionally contributed to the rent that has been capitalised into my property through their contribution to the Jubilee Line funding. *For the present I choose to repay their generosity by keeping the rents to the pre-Jubilee Line levels. However, if I were to sell my firm at market value, a new owner of the properties would immediately raise the rents to current local values to get a market rate of return, which at present is about 8% on my type of commercial property.*

Ten years ago I started to compile notes for a book that would be entitled *How to Succeed in Property*. I was able to draw on memorable dealings with my fellow property speculators in Southwark and elsewhere, whom I met at auctions. At the auctions of residential property, many of the speculators talked and acted like Kray twin enforcers. Up the social scale, at commercial property sales, or meetings in estate agents' offices or on sites, I met more polished operators who had been born into the property business, or had joined a syndicate or had been promoted away from levering out sitting tenants. I learned a great deal from meeting and listening to these rogues. After all, they are only operating within the rules that we, as electors, have mandated our MPs to enshrine in laws. However, I now knew that the spectacular fortunes made by many property developers were often due to society's failure to collect its dues, and that the primary point of my *How to Succeed in Property* book would have to acknowledge this – and only then spell out the hard work and know-how that would not be much different from *How to Succeed in Any Business*.

But my investigation into where the taxpayers' money ended up as a result of transport investment could just as easily be titled *Where the taxpayers' money did not end up*. For example, certain classes of employment should bear a *Public Health Warning*, such as those in which citizens hope to combine a career in public service with a fair standard of residential accommodation located near their work. Since the Second World War, successive Ministers of Finance right down to Gordon Brown have used wage freezes, retail price indexes and downright cheating when calculating statistics to hold down public pay increases to about a half that of average house price inflation. The implications should be obvious from the earlier chapters of this book. The people whose work enhances the wealth of surrounding communities are fined or penalised by those same citizens who benefit from good local schools, regular transport, hospitals and an alert, well- staffed constabulary. Thus teachers, Tube and rail workers, nurses and police are unable to afford accommodation where they work, in areas where they have helped to push up property (more precisely, land) prices![1]

Citizens whose properties have risen in value under Labour by more than the 50% as part of the general demand, plus an additional 20 to 40% due to better public facilities, simply bless their foresight or good luck and ignore their role as voters in creating the wretchedness imposed on employees who are unlucky enough to be employed in the public sector. As *Guardian* reporter Charlotte Denny wrote: "Private sector employers could not get away with this kind of tight-fistedness, but because the government is a monopoly employer when it comes to teaching and nursing in state schools and hospitals, it is able to artificially suppress wages".[2]

---

[1] Caroline McGhie, "Property rises by 50%, *Sunday Telegraph*, January 16, 2000.
[2] Charlotte Denny, "Public Pay Lag", *The Guardian*, March 22, 2001.

The earlier chapters of the book were devoted to proving that transport can be privately funded, privately run and staffed by employees who are private sector employees. I hope that this short book will stimulate others to analyse other existing "public" sectors such as schools and hospitals to demonstrate how these, too, could be privately financed and run without being a cross hanging around the throats of taxpayers. In particular, the trades unions that represent public sector employees ought to deploy their research departments on a project of fundamental research to independently document the case that I have made. Then, they ought to mobilise their members behind a serious campaign of reform to persuade New Labour to give a new meaning to the concept of a public-private partnership. That would be the most effective way to raise their members' living standards – and to take a great deal of the aggro out of politics.

The gains for landowners from improvements in the transport system are no more than the icing on the cake. Sitting on top of the economy there is a huge iceberg of rental income. How this revenue is created and shared is the key to understanding the way in which the economy works (or, very often, *fails* to work). The story of two sites will drive home this point.

Twenty years ago I bought a vacant site in Borough High Street, 300 yards south of what would one day become the location for a station on the Jubilee Underground line. It was a site of 2,000 square feet and I paid the owner, Frys Properties, £10 a square foot – a total of £20,000. Today, that land is worth about £200 a sq. foot.

I wanted to construct something that would enhance the fabric of the commercial environment. So, I drove into the Suffolk countryside in search of materials for a building that would have character. I bought a disused 16th century oak-framed barn from a farmer in the village of Diss and transported the material back to London. The result was 169A Borough High Street, complete with exposed beams.

The novel building became an architectural attraction. I used it as offices for small businesses. In those two decades, I estimate that my tenants and I have contributed something like £700,000 to the local and central government budgets as property tax, corporation tax, payroll

Don's utterly magnificent (and crazy) 16th century barn just behind Borough High Street. As a testimony to Don's creativity, it looks in keeping with the area, like a magical part of London that's escaped the developers. In truth, it's magic created by a visionary developer who cared about the location and spirit of the area he was developing.

tax, and the rest of the fiscal burdens imposed on people who earn their living. At least two tenants have gone on to buy their own buildings, so successful were they.

My piece of land was put to good use *despite* the opposition from government-sponsored tax policies, which are calculated to deter people (*see Box 9:1*). Meanwhile, other owners left their sites idle.

Example: from a window in my beamed building, I would gaze at the site on the other side of the road, at what would be 116–126 Borough High Street.

For 20 years, that site remained a dead asset to the community. Vacant. While I was repaying the loans on the land purchase and on the construction of my building, and we were paying our taxes related to it, the vacant site irritated me every day.

Don's 169A Borough High Street development from further down the alleyway.

Box 9:1
The Tax Vortex

The link between bad tax policy and property is illustrated in the US where governments acquire property in place of the unpaid taxes that are, in part, responsible for causing idle land in the first place. The degeneration of the urban environment that results from penal taxes is illustrated in the tragedy of Detroit, where the city government found itself in possession of about 45,000 parcels of real estate due to unpaid taxes.

Many of the buildings and sites were vacant at a time when land prices were rocketing in the late 1990s (by 20% in 1999), but builders could not get enough land on which to construct homes and retail properties. Government tax policy is at the vortex of the economic hurricane that blights human settlements.

According to the "Clean Slate" Jubilee as it was inherited from Mesopotamia, and recorded in the Old Testament, debts that stemmed from government action should be periodically cancelled and the land returned to the people who had been dispossessed. But in Detroit, the red tape was so dense that the people who would use the vacant sites to renew the blighted districts were defeated by bureaucracy.*

* Christopher Bowe, "Recent history's ills slowly being cured", *Financial Times* (supplement: Detroit region), 28 February, 2000.

In 1980 it was available for purchase for around £100,000. In January 2000 it was sold for £2.6 million. *The site failed to contribute to the economy and the welfare of the residents of Southwark, but it was "money in the bank" for the owners. They only had to pick their time to sell it and realise the value buried in the land.*

If that site and others like it were put to use, the community would be raised to a higher level of prosperity. Unfortunately, our tax system is biased against people who work, and it rewards people who keep valuable land idle. Ironically, when government tries to remedy the problem through tax policy, they actually make matters worse (*see Box 9:2*).

But it is important to realise that it is not the motive to speculate that is the problem. Efficiency in the consumer and capital markets is enhanced by people who trade as prices go up and down. Resources are reallocated and prices are levelled off within narrower limits. It is when the Treasury encourages hoarding in the land market that the society-wide problems occur. That is when the private pursuit of unearned income creates public crises, and the liability is shifted on to taxpayers.

An original picture from the first edition showing 116–126 Borough High Street. Land owners doing nothing with a site except counting their gains as others improve an area.

This is the site today, a combined retail and residential – office block.

The problem remains though with holes in the high street. This is a few doors from Don's building on his side of the road.

Box 9:2
Brown's Brownfield Bonanza

The government wants Britain's builders to construct more houses on urban brownfield sites.

Gordon Brown, the Chancellor of the Exchequer, gave us a taste of what he called his "vision for the future of the tax system" when he changed the tax rules in his budget on March 7, 2001.

"To make the first stages of buying property and bringing land back into use tax free, in designated areas stamp duty will be abolished," he told the House of Commons. "To bring disused properties back into use, we will cut VAT on residential property conversions from 17.5% to 5%."

Mr. Brown does not understand that the tax cuts will be capitalised into higher land prices. Prospective developers in the deprived areas of cities would not be required to pay less for land because of the tax cuts.

The Treasury ought to have learnt from the Thatcher experiment with the tax-free Enterprise Zones of the 1980s: land values shot up by the amount of the tax "benefits".

Under the Treasury rules, landowners are always ahead of the game ...

The correct discipline for the land market is to not relieve land of tax, but transfer the tax burden off people's wages and savings and on to their land.

Private property owners behave rationally within the legal rules of the game. Their social responsibilities are no more or less than yours or mine. If they can maximise their wealth by keeping land idle for a couple of decades while the community grows around them, they are acting prudently in their best private interests.

It is important to realise, however, that the public sector is equally guilty of freezing valuable sites out of use; and for that, there can be no excuse. Governments are charged by their electorates with a duty to uphold the public interest. Politicians get elected by promising to do a better job than the other lot. So when they keep land vacant, vacillating over how to put it to good commercial or social use, there can be few excuses.

Example: a prime site by the river overlooking Eel Pie Island, which is famous for one of the early venues of the Rolling Stones in the 1960s.

The swimming pool that occupied the site in Twickenham, Middlesex, was closed more than 20 years ago. Despite two property cycles during those two decades, the councillors of the London borough of Richmond upon Thames failed to maximise the financial or the social benefits of that plum piece of land for the benefit of their rate payers. The government's Best Value instruction to local governments applies insufficient pressure on councillors to put these sites to use as fast as people need them. The council admits that "Best Value requires authorities to review and examine all their services every five years to ensure they meet the needs of residents".[3] But, meanwhile, the value of those sites goes to waste.

Riverside locations such as the one in Twickenham command high premiums from people willing to pay over the odds to live beside water. Alternatively, such a site could provide commercial and recreational facilities that would attract people into the town centre for the benefit of shopkeepers. Instead, the site remains an eyesore which blights the waterfront walkway. And over those 20 years, revenue that could have gone into the coffers of the rate payers was flushed down the Thames and into the North Sea, never to be recovered.

Private owners can justify behaving in ways that are not illegal, but the same defence cannot be offered for public agencies that exercise authority over the nation's scarcest of resources – land. They have, by definition, a *public duty* to uphold the public interest.

If that site and the other ones like it were put to use, the community would be raised to a higher level of prosperity.

Unfortunately, our tax system is biased against people who work, and it rewards people who keep valuable land idle.

One of the scandals that needs to be exposed is the way in which governments and their statistical agencies resolutely refuse to chronicle that waste in the land market (*see Box 9:3*). If you look for official figures for vacant land in our cities, you won't find them. Academics occasionally hazard guesses, but governments fail to see the need to monitor the failures in the turnover of land-sites. Instead, they fixate over unemployment in the labour market. And yet, according to the London Development Agency:

---

[3] London Borough of Richmond upon Thames, *Best Value Performance Plan 2001/2002*, March 2001, p.2.

The lack of suitable development land and premises is frequently cited in business surveys as an impediment to growth ... London's industrial stock tends to be older, poorly managed and poorly serviced than other regions. With some notable exceptions, start up businesses take accommodation which is unsuited to their needs and, frequently, works against their long term ability to expand.[4]

The artificial shortage of land and premises is primarily caused by the faulty tax system. But you would never know it, looking at the Treasury's statistics on trends in the economy. It is easy to be misled by heartrending stories about planning permission delays, and to assume that it is too severe planning regulation that stifles the initiatives of individuals and building companies. However, the earlier chapters of this book should have made it clear that the planners, too, are victims of a system that is *forced to adapt* to our faulty tax system. Planners have no financial yardstick because the systematic provision of land data is not made available, with which to measure the value of competing uses of the same or different sites for the community.

[4] London Development Agency, *Draft Economic Development Strategy*, London, November 2000, p. 30.

Box 9:3
Where's the Land Price Index?

As an insider in the property market, I have the advantage of living with land prices, which signal when the market is going up, down or sideways.

Governments are not so well informed. In fact, they are seriously misled by their favourite tracking devices. Take "house" prices, whose movements actually reflect swift shifts in land values – not bricks-and- mortars. In Britain, even house price data is confusing. The two leading indexes are published by Nationwide (the biggest building society) and Halifax, the mortgage bank. When the going gets rough, they tend to mislead Bank of England economists who set interest rates. In February 2001, as the financial markets went into meltdown, the Bank of England was told that house asset values had

- soared by 11.2% over the previous year – Nationwide; but
- weakened so much that the rise was only 0.9% – Halifax.[1]

What is a banker to do on the basis of such confusion?
Britain needs a sensitively constructed land price index that identifies regional and sectoral trends. The Inland Revenue's Valuation Department does publish data; but too late to affect week-to-week policy-making by the Treasury and Bank of England. The Department of the Environment's land price data is of use to historians, but that is about all.

But data without theoretical insight is not much use, either.

For more than 100 years, New Zealand has tracked land values for fiscal purposes. In recent decades, governments have chosen to ignore the warning signals flashed by the land market.[2]

Japan has an excellent government statistical agency that collates land values down to precinct levels. But during the 1990s, ideology came before economic insight: governments chose to ignore the lessons of the land market – which explains why Japan has suffered a decade-long slump.

Australia has good land-value data, but its politicians continue to flirt with fashionable economic doctrines while neglecting the understanding – brought to the shores by settlers – that rental income is the primary source of public finance. That is why, over the next 20 years, the gap between the rich and the poor will continue to widen – with the landowners as the winners.[3]

1 David Turner, "Mortgage lenders at odds over house values", *Financial Times*, Feb. 7, 2001.
2 Ron Ward, "Economic prediction and the Asian crisis", *Land & Liberty*, Spring 1999, p.8.
3 Tony O'Brien, "The Pathology of Income Maldistribution", Geophilos, Autumn 2000, No.00(1), pp.44–69.

Foreign evidence provides an impression of the scale of the problem. Is the information any better in the United States? The US Bureau of the Census does not collect data on the use of land. Thirty years ago the scale of the waste of land in cities was estimated.[5] In the intervening years – nothing! But two scholars recently undertook a survey to measure the scale of vacancy. The results are summarised in Table 9:1.

Table 9:1 Vacant Land and Abandoned Buildings, USA (1998)*			
Census Region	Av'ge Vacant Land (acres)	Vacant Land in Av'ge % of total Land Area	Av'ge No. of Abandoned Structures per 1,000 Inhabitants
Cities Reporting	12,376	15.4	2.63
South	20,011	19.3	2.98
West	10,349	14.8	0.62
Midwest	5,904	12.2	3.16
Northeast	5,004	9.6	7.47

* Derived from Michael A. Pagano & Ann O'M Bowman, *Vacant Land in Cities: An Urban Resource*, Brookings Institution Center on Urban & Metropolitan Policy, December, 2000, Tables 2 & 3, pp. 6–7.

This information is based on a private survey which revealed massive waste. Of the 70 cities with populations of more than 100,000 that were surveyed, the average per cent of vacant land was 15.4%. The cities in the South hoard far greater quantities of vacant land, but this does not mean that the largest cities of the Northeast are more prudent. For they have the larger number of abandoned structures, which represents vacant land and capital tied up in the form of buildings going begging.

The Federal government does not quantify this waste. So, it is not surprising to learn that only 56% of the cities used a computerised system to track vacant land. And yet, the local communities and their economies are crippled to an extent that in some cases defies imagination.

- Philadelphia reported that it had 36.5 abandoned structures per 1,000 population.
- Phoenix reported approximately 128,000 acres of vacant land, which is 43% of land within the city.

[5] Reported in Harrison, *The Power in the Land*, p.216.

But these round numbers fail to provide anything like the correct impression of what is happening on the ground. The spatial loss can be measured, in terms of acres and square miles, but this snapshot, by itself, does not tell the full truth about the economic damage to the economy; nor does it convey an impression of the ecological waste and damage which is inflicted on the natural environment as a result of urban sprawl.

Vacant land with or without unoccupied buildings is a crude measure of the waste. However, for every site surrounded by car park signs there are scores more hoarded sites disguised by buildings on them that are long past their prime use dates. These properties are cheap to hoard because the buildings have negligible value compared to the land, and thus conventional property taxes are low (*see Box 9:4*). You only have to look at the valuable sites that are "employed" as temporary car parks to realise that owners are depriving their cities of the full benefits of strategically located tracts of land.

Why do owners – which includes local and central governments – waste land on this scale? In the case of land owned by public sector agencies, the explanation is probably one of inertia. In the case of private owners, the main motive is speculation. This emerges dramatically in the US data. The largest amounts of vacant land were to be found in the growing cities in the South and West. This is where we would expect to observe speculation in the raw: land is hoarded in the expectation of urban growth. The owners anticipate large capital gains in the future, as people move into the city, so it pays them to keep their sites vacant for as long as possible. The result of this is a leap-frogging process of development, in which cities expand into the countryside at a rate that exceeds what is required by the people moving into them.

> *"The Capital Gains Tax system is now so complex as to be almost unworkable. Many businesses say they and their accountants are just unable to work out their CGT liabilities."*
>
> – Chris Humphries, Director-General,
> British Chambers of Commerce

Box 9:4
Footprints in Seattle

Towns and cities ought to renew themselves spontaneously. Such an organic evolution would ensure that the built environment fitted neatly with the needs of citizens.

Instead, the tax system is a positive (bad) feedback mechanism which perpetuates stagnation. The political response, when governments get round to it, is a built environment that sits uneasily with the needs of residents. Either we get soulless residential estates, or a lopsided concentration of commercial structures that are hostile to local liveable communities.

The under-use of land is heavily concealed by buildings which are seriously under-employed. The footprints of the speculators sometimes only come to the public's attention with the death of people like Sam Israel in Seattle, Washington, in the northwest corner of the United States.

Across the street from Pike Place Market, where land is worth $100 a square foot, almost an entire block is made up of parking lots and derelict buildings. Much of the block is part of the empire assembled by Sam Israel, who owned 40 parcels and dozens of sites elsewhere. After his death in 1994, the *Seattle Times* noted: "He owned more property in downtown Seattle – and had done less with it – than any other private landowner in the city".

The economic impact was recorded by two authors who noted: "holding his 5.4 acres of prime urban sites out of full development meant pushing thousands of offices, apartments, and shops out of the urban core".

The authors identified the remedy. "Land speculation is parasitic, not productive. Its antidote is to shift the property tax off buildings and on to land. Exempting buildings from the property tax and shifting its full burden on to land values would have put Sam Israel out of business – or into the business of developing premium sites rather than hoarding them. It would have boosted his Seattle tax bill by $200,000 a year, eliminating almost all the profits he might have hoped for from land value appreciation. To pay the tax, he would have had to generate more income by developing or selling some of his parcels."*

The efficient public collection of rent would turn land values into signals of confidence in people's locations. Residents would be able to directly fund the services they wanted. Where land values were low, these would galvanise residents into focusing attention on potential improvement to their communities which would start with better use of their land.

* A.T. Durning & Y. Bauman, *Tax Shift*, Seattle: Northwest Environment Watch, 1998, pp. 61, 62.

The failings of the land market surface in many forms. One is the implosion of cities as businesses are driven out of the centres by unaffordable rents. In the residential districts of old-established cities, we see the collapse of communities for the same reason: families find they are priced out of centrally located areas. This, in turn, leads to social fragmentation. The middle classes flee to the suburbs, and the low-income families are concentrated in ghettos or subsidised public housing.

I would have thought that this was a process that would be closely monitored by local governments. And yet, the US study found that of the 99 cities that responded, only 60 could estimate the number of abandoned structures within their borders. The authors correctly state:

> Without a reliable data base containing information about derelict property throughout a city or a formal data collecting process, a systematic response to vacant land will prove elusive … many cities also indicated that they had designed no policies for encouraging the use or re-use of city-owned vacant land and abandoned structures.[6]

This is dereliction of public duty on a massive scale, and yet it escapes public censure. Why? In the main, political philosophy remains silent about the significance of land. And economic theory in the last century found a way to rationalise the waste in the land market so that unused sites would not be condemned as a failure of public policy.[7]

Waste in the land market is the direct responsibility of the way in which government chooses to tax – or, more precisely, not to tax – our land. This raises the important issue that economists and social reformers ought to take into account.

Generally, when people observe problems such as the large-scale waste of land in cities, they blame "the market". Environmentalists attribute responsibility to something they call "market failure".[8]

[6] Pagano & Bowman, *Ibid.*, p.8.
[7] Mason Gaffney, "Neo-classical Economics as a Stratagem against Henry George", in M. Gaffney & F. Harrison, *The Corruption of Economics*, London: Shepheard-Walwyn, 1994, pp. 82–103.
[8] Joe Ravetz, *City Region 2020: Integrated Planning for a Sustainable Development*, London: Earthscan, 2000, p.236.

Take a closer look. Actions that appear socially irrational are rational from the point of view of people's personal interests. People can only act on the basis of the laws and conventions ordained by society. They are entitled to express their personal preferences within the rules of the social game. Those rules are established by a democratically-elected parliament. Therefore, if landowners (say) willfully withhold land from the market, even when there is a huge demand for it, they are doing what comes naturally: maximising their capital gains. They are behaving legally and sensibly; for them, the market is operating efficiently.

Now, if – from society's viewpoint – we do not like the end-result, it is futile to vent anger on "the market". *Blame the people who make the rules.* It is the political class, in the end, that sets the framework for what is permissible, and what is not allowed. If the laws of the land facilitate anti-social behaviour – change the laws! In other words, we are dealing with "political failure", not market failure. As voters, we all have the right to demand change. If we fail to insist on our democratic rights, in defence of our natural rights, then we have to live with the consequences – but it is unreasonable to shift responsibility onto "the market".

In this study, I have directed blame at HM Treasury for its failure to innovate appropriate reforms: it is the guardian of economic orthodoxy. It is schooled to preserve the present rules, and champion the system for raising public revenue, which is the direct cause of the chaos in the markets. Take, for example, the way in which local government raises revenue through taxation on people's real estate.

- Council Tax and Business Rates are charges on buildings as well as land. As such, they penalise people and firms for putting buildings on land.
- Vacant sites are exempted. This compromises performance in the economy, and reduces the taxable surplus available to the public sector.

We can summarise the problem in one sentence: *the privatisation of rent corrupts the productive capacity of the economy, and corrupts the fibre of public life.*

The complement of this perversion of public finance is the socialisation of people's private (earned) incomes. This is an abuse of people's rights, and yet we celebrate it with strange rituals in parliament, when the chancellor presents his annual budget, as if the government was abiding by norms of rationality.

As a result, people's economic and social prospects are savagely curtailed, which turns many of them into dependent clients on the public and on the goodwill of government.

This failure of public policy is disastrous for people trying to make a living. For the primary signals in the market are prices. Where to allocate resources, how much to buy, how much to save for one's retirement, the amount that can be safely earmarked for recreation – everything depends on a correct assessment of what the pricing mechanism tells us. And when this mechanism is encrusted with tax charges, some of which are deliberately concealed from the public, and which are subject to arbitrary change at the whim of the Treasury, the market is not being fine-tuned by signals but is being bombarded by noise.

And then, when the market appears to fail – thanks to government interference – the cry of anguish that goes up leads to demands for democratic action. In steps the plodding politician with regulations and "rescue packages" to remedy the problems which they created in the first place!

All of this is like telling the pilot of a jumbo jet to land at Heathrow by flying through a gigantic magnetic force. All the dials on the instruments panel are sent haywire. The pilot's vision is already distorted – he cannot see the ground beneath him – and the dials are supposed to provide sophisticated guidance that enables him to operate with precision. Instead, he is even worse off: the dials are actually feeding him misinformation. Would you trust an airline that put your life at that kind of risk? I do not think so. But we live with that kind of interference from the Treasury, and we do nothing about it.

"Mr. Brown might also think about simplifying taxes. His incessant tinkering bemuses experts and annoys businessmen: his last Finance Bill weighed in at 558 pages. There are now five income tax bands, 15 rates of capital gains tax, 21 rates of company car tax and hundreds of exemptions and allowances from corporation tax."
– *Financial Times*, February 26, 2001

The philosophy of governance has to be fine-tuned to the realities of life. The fundamental reform is to erase all the distortions that governments impose on the economy and society. The first step is to shift the tax burden off people.

By applying the commonsense rule of charging people for the benefits they receive from the occupation of land, government would be armed with the most powerful anti-cyclical policy. The boom/bust cycle is mainly driven by the pursuit of capital gains from land. By applying the benefits-received principle, there would be little or no land-rent left to capitalise into unearned gains. That would leave people free to concentrate on value-adding enterprise.

In the South East of England, the periodic housing booms that are a drag on the regions would be killed off. We now know that monetary policy attempts to control house price bubbles are a failure.

In the relatively deprived regions of the North, the tax burden would be reduced to levels that people could afford. That would automatically lead to the revival of localities without the need for complex bureaucratic controls or the dead hand of the Treasury.

Under the present Treasury orthodoxy, dying communities such as those to be found on the East side of the centre of Manchester can only be rescued under the paternalistic guidance of government. In fact, the scale of the problem is so enormous that politicians and bureaucrats cannot hope to provide the solution. A study from Birmingham University reveals that 280,000 homes along the M62 corridor between Manchester and Merseyside are blighted. This is 17% of properties, including almost 100,000 private houses. Houses that were bought for £34,000 at the peak of the housing boom in 1988 cannot now be sold for £10,000 in Salford.[9]

Economically marginalised areas require the power of the market (which means the collective efforts of everybody acting rationally), linked to a rational public finance system, to rescue them. Land values in these areas are all but zero. This means that commercial and residential occupants ought to be paying virtually nothing for occupying the land. But nor should they be penalised by the Treasury when they buy their clothes and groceries.

The conclusion is unavoidable: a public revenue system that integrates land and taxation is a sophisticated combination that provides the rapid

---

[9] Peter Hetherington, "Trapped in the property wastelands", *The Guardian*, March 7, 2001.

response to both economic disturbances and social renewal, and it lays the foundations for a sustainable economics, which under the present rules is beyond our grasp.

2024 Update

Don mentions a number of empty sites in the book and in this chapter in particular. At a local level, the undeveloped site that was literally across the road from Don's remarkable timber framed building on Borough High Street was eventually developed. However, undeveloped gaps remain on the high street in Borough and all over London, and landlords are not punished for withholding investment.

At a national level, for at least a decade, long-term empty properties declined steadily across the UK from over 300,000 dwellings to nearly 200,000 in 2016. Unfortunately, there's been a steady rise since and the latest available figures stand at 260,000 empty dwellings.

Unsurprisingly, there's a concentration in London. Campaign group *Action on Empty Homes* (AEH) reported that in the City of London, 1 in 3 dwellings is classified as long-term empty. In Southwark, Don's area of interest, it was 1 in 24, which in real terms is an estimated 3,600 empty homes. This excludes land that that could be used for social housing. Over the whole city, there are over 100,000 homes in London that are empty. This could be much higher as people are able to reclassify their empty houses as second homes and take them off the list.

As with most political issues around our land and property market, plenty of politicians say useful sounding things but little actually happens when you follow up to see if they actually did anything. https://www.actiononemptyhomes.org/nobody-home

One of AEH's research findings is that homes that are built in London tend to be for second homes and Airbnb-ready flats. There is less development to meet local needs. One other charity that campaigns for fairer housing is Trust for London. https://trustforlondon.org.uk/

Their aims would resonate deeply with Don's anger, which he expressed in this chapter about why Gordon Brown allowed the housing market to overheat, and doing so whilst limiting public sector pay increases. The result of which meant that those who helped make their city better couldn't afford to live there.

One interesting example of some of the challenges of developing old sites is the former swimming pool site opposite Eel Pie Island in Twickenham. This remained derelict for a long time. In 2003, a collaboration between the council and residents made improvements and it was turned into a public space that is now much loved by the residents.

In 2011, the incoming Conservative Council turned the land over to a residents' organisation, the Twickenham Riverside Trust. They were given a 125-year lease in exchange for taking care of it. The site is now called the Diamond Jubilee Gardens.

In 2018, a newly elected Liberal Democrat Council then tried to retake the land and even issued a compulsory purchase order in 2021 for the site. Their plan is to build apartments on the site and include public space and a promenade. Resident groups, led by the Riverside Trust, have fought this. At time of publication, all sides are awaiting the outcome of a public enquiry into the legality of the compulsory purchase order and whether the plans can go ahead.

Celia Holman, Secretary of the Trust, said, "The Diamond Jubilee Gardens has become a true community site used today by dozens of groups of all ages. The current site is used by several nurseries as their outdoor space. We have lots of exercise groups from football to tai chi and we run approximately a dozen events a year in the gardens. We believe all this generates a halo uplift to the surrounding area. We would love to work with the council to enhance and improve the land they already own that they have left derelict. Unfortunately, they seem more interested in the development of private flats."

There is a recording of an interview by local radio with the leader of the local council, Gareth Roberts, and the head of the Trust, Ted Cremin in the following link:

https://www.twickenhamriversidetrust.org/riverside-development

The situation in Twickenham demonstrates another crucial aspect to land value economics. The sites that enhance space for many people are often open ones. They give everyone space to breathe. However, the undoubted value they create both in psychological and economic terms by making an area more desirable (and so increasing house and land values) isn't captured by the council. Therefore, if they want to capture those gains, they must do so in another way. The compulsory purchase of a site that is held in trust by the community is an extreme way to capture the land value. If we had a tax system that allowed the gains from renovation of public and derelict land to be reinvested in the community, there could be more democratic ways to develop space, or for a community to prefer to leave a space open because it benefited everyone.

Postscript by Dave Wetzel
Former vice Chair Transport for London

Picture taken at the launch of Don's book in 2001 with Simon Hughes MP (for Bermondsey and Old Southwark) and Dave Wetzel and Don Riley.
© https://cooperative-individualism.org/land-and-liberty_mp-endorses-message-in-don-riley's-taken-for-a-ride-2001-jul-sep.pdf

There cannot be many people who can claim a book they've written has changed government policy and the economic geography of a major city – but Don Riley's *Taken for a Ride* did just that for London.

I didn't share Don Riley's politics. In fact, his hand-written inscription in my copy of his book reads, *"To Dave. We agree on more than we disagree! Don R."* This is true. Unlike me, Don was no Green socialist. He wanted much less government. But his fundamental truths, that: ***"all practical and desirable transport projects could (and should) be funded from the wealth they generate in land values"*** and that ***"people***

should pay for the benefits they receive". These truths are messages for politicians of all political hues.

I strongly recommend this book, for although Don Riley wrote it over twenty years ago, the opening of the Elizabeth Underground Line in 2022, and the start of HS2, the High-Speed railway line from Euston to Birmingham and beyond, makes his message even more apposite and relevant today.

As Vice Chair of Transport for London (TfL) I often cited the ideas and the numbers Don reveals in this book at meetings with politicians, journalists, transport experts, academics, landowners, developers, town planners, government officers, finance specialists, and particularly the Treasury. My efforts mostly fell on deaf ears, but eventually did begin to strike a chord. Let me give a specific example. In 2001, TfL approached the UK Government for the funding required to build Crossrail (now the Elizabeth Line). The Treasury continually refused permission for an annual Land Value Tax to finance Crossrail. However, together with London Mayor Ken Livingstone and Bob Kiley (our American Transport Commissioner), we persevered and proposed a "supplementary business rate" based on the existing UK's property tax on commercial premises. This was eventually agreed and levied on the more expensive business premises in the London area. This would finance a quarter of the costs of Crossrail.

As Don explains in his book, the optimum solution would have been for all the landowners, who massively benefit financially from Crossrail, to contribute the total capital cost of building the new line via an annual Land Value Tax.

Of course, it is not just the building of a new railway that creates increased land values, as long as the trains continue to be operated on these new lines, so do the increased rents continue to flow as an unearned income into the pockets of passive landowners. This rental income should rightly be used to maintain the services, to pay good wages to rail workers, and to charge travellers modest or even no fares – imagine this impact on pollution, the environment, and climate change as people leave their cars at home!

It was only many years later when speaking to a former senior Treasury official that I learnt that *Taken for a Ride* and the supplementary rate idea were the "game changers", the deciding factors that enabled Alistair Darling, the new Labour Chancellor, to sign off on Crossrail.

The ideas in *Taken for a Ride* would improve communities, increase prosperity, create fairness, promote hard work and entrepreneurialism, and help almost all members of society. Yet, the question remains, why has this still not changed?

I can see the success Crossrail is already bringing to the region. And I can also see the cost of all the compromises that the taxpayers (served by TfL and the government) had to make just to get the project going. For example, back in the mid-2000s to take ownership of key sites so that they could start the building work, they had to agree to a demand from the incumbent landowners that, whilst they could buy the buildings (and demolish them for construction of the line), the original landowner still had the rights to the air above the existing building! As hard as this is to believe, it's true.

What this meant in functional terms was that when the area warranted and even benefitted from a much taller building, Crossrail could only rebuild to the height of the building that was demolished. They then had to hand the building back to the original owners. This means the landowner could then build much more profitably themselves at a later date.

Further, local authorities also insisted that Crossrail "rebuild in conformity" with what was there before. For instance, at Tottenham Court Road on the Westminster side, a theatre was replaced even though it appeared to have little commercial value. Londoners will be familiar with a large building at Tottenham Court Road called Centre Point. Centre Point has 35 stories and is currently being renovated by Almacantar Ltd., an exclusive property developer, and Conran and Partners, one of the world's top design firms. A 2100 ft^2 apartment costs £8m. Another tall building would have been perfectly acceptable and desirable, generating several hundred million pounds that could have been used to finance Crossrail.

https://centrepointresidences.co.uk/apartments/

Challenges with incumbent landowners and the local authorities led to expensive compromises. This then leaves us with the first and final obstacle to a worthwhile transport project – the Treasury. I remember well my interactions and obstacles with the Treasury working to fund Crossrail. And for more on the issues with the Treasury, reread Steve Norris's experiences of having to threaten to attack the then prime minister, John Major just to get them to approve the project.

I have worked with other transport specialists around the world, and they find our approach to transport projects inexplicable. Leaders in places like Hong Kong or Singapore can't imagine the taxpayer paying so much only for the gains to go to private investors who did nothing to help.

Had Don's suggestions been implemented, we could have built the Jubilee Line Extension in a way that paid for Crossrail, which could have paid for Crossrail 2, and so on. Politicians and the public would have had to take a generational view of a project and not just a parliamentary or even a news cycle view of things, and it would have had a transformational effect. All we have to do is build a railway AND consider other developments around the stations simultaneously.

Transport planners and politicians, considering the value of proposed, competing transport projects face many obstacles often requiring the calculation of theoretical "value for money", "cost-social benefit" and "saved journey times" valued differently for rich and poor people. Significantly, Don Riley examines how assessing future land values would allow planners and decision-makers to identify the value that society gives each scheme. If some schemes create more land value than they cost, then they should be the projects to consider carefully. This is because the increase in land value is an amalgam of all those different economic decisions that we in society make on a daily basis.

If one takes a longer-term view of Don's ideas, we can see that he was not the first to suggest funding public transport from land values. In this book, he has cited many academics, and others. Don stands out because, to my knowledge, he was the first who offered his unique perspective as a beneficial businessman and a landowner.

Twenty years before the publication of this book, as Chair of the Greater London Council's Transport Committee in 1981, we worked jointly with the London Docklands Development Corporation to develop the Docklands Light Railway. I suggested we compulsorily purchased all the land surrounding each of the new stations before we announced their location, but I was advised by the GLC's solicitors that we didn't have the power to do this – so the existing landowners made a fortune from our public funding of the railway.

Frank Pick, who held my position as Deputy Chair of London Transport in the 1930s gave evidence to Parliament in 1938 where he pointed out that once a new underground line was announced, land values would skyrocket. Consequently, he suggested that London Transport should become a land speculator and let others take all the risks of building lines and running the trains!

If you travel in London, you'll see Frank Pick's work every day. He was responsible for the stunning London Underground bull's-eye symbol, Harry Beck's Underground map, the Johnston typeface unique to LT, and the beautiful art-deco posters and stations of the 1930s. He was a man of deep integrity and was committed to a life of public service. He even turned down a peerage and other honours, as it went against his values.

Whenever I have mentioned changing the tax system it's pointed out to me that homeowners would be understandably upset at having to pay more through their properties/land they own. This is a misunderstanding as this increase in one tax would be matched with a reduction in income taxes and other deadweight taxes. These changes would create a much fairer system and lower taxes for the overwhelming majority, as people would keep more of the money they make, and they would be rewarded for creating a vibrant community.

The real reason anything to do with a change in land/property taxes becomes so controversial is that the people who control the mainstream media are in the small group who would pay more tax. Consequently, they ensure the press is extremely hostile to the idea, and this prevents the measured debate we desperately need. Without that conversation, the public will be unable to make an informed choice between an increase in land/property taxes AND a massive reduction in other taxes.

Over the years, politicians have said with almost religious fervour that you don't mess with land or property taxes (think Thatcher and the poll tax). Politicians in office won't go near it. Only when they are retired do politicians suggest a change to a fairer tax and economic system. Tony Blair is the latest high-profile politician to do this through one of his charities. If he'd had the courage to speak up when he was in office, Crossrail may have improved the South for over 10 years instead of 12 months, and our public finances may have been in a much better state than they are now.

It comes back to the (possibly apocryphal) quote from a politician, "I know what the right thing to do is, but I just don't know how to get elected after I've done it."

We are left with an economic system that is unfair, in which people are punished for doing the right thing. Attempts to improve the lives of ordinary people are met with relentless criticism. The idea that the Jubilee Line investments were seen as unnecessary or not worth the cost is incredible today, given the extraordinary way in which it transformed London. The same criticisms are presented to Crossrail and any other investment that improves normal people's lives. What Don's book, *Taken for a Ride*, and all research since has shown is that not only are they worthwhile, but they serve all of us. We live on a planet where all the benefits from the economy and land were once shared by all. Today that equitable and just system has been usurped by landowners who provide nothing to the production process except permission for someone else to do the work.

It's up to all of us, of whatever political persuasion, to introduce fairness, harmony and most importantly – justice – in our economic system.